Architectural Design
November/December 2008

Neoplasmatic Design

Guest-edited by Marcos Cruz and Steve Pike

IN THIS ISSUE

Main Section

WILEY
wiley.com

Architectural Design

Vol 78 No 6
ISBN 978-0470 51958 5

Editorial Offices
John Wiley & Sons
International House
Ealing Broadway Centre
London W5 5DB

T: +44 (0)20 8326 3800

Editor
Helen Castle

Regular columnists: Valentina Croci, David
Littlefield, Jayne Merkel, Will McLean, Neil
Spiller, Michael Weinstock and Ken Yeang

Freelance Managing Editor
Caroline Ellerby

Production Editor
Elizabeth Gongde

Design and Prepress
Artmedia Press, London

Printed in Italy by Conti Tipocolor

Sponsorship/advertising
Faith Pidduck/Wayne Frost
T: +44 (0)1243 770254
E: fpidduck@wiley.co.uk

Front cover: Samuel White (Unit 20, Bartlett
School of Architecture, UCL), Cellular Growth
Enhancement, 2003-04. Views from within a
Petri dish in which the growth of human skin
cells is enhanced with the help of micro-
machinery. © Samuel White

Subscribe to ⚏

⚏ is published bimonthly and is available to
purchase on both a subscription basis and as
individual volumes at the following prices.

PRICES
Individual copies: £22.99/$45.00
Mailing fees may apply

ANNUAL SUBSCRIPTION RATES
Student: UK£70/US$110 print only
Individual: UK £110/US$170 print only
Institutional: UK£180/US$335 print or online
Institutional: UK£198/US$369 combined print
and online

Subscription Offices UK
John Wiley & Sons Ltd
Journals Administration Department
1 Oldlands Way, Bognor Regis
West Sussex, PO22 9SA
T: +44 (0)1243 843272
F: +44 (0)1243 843232
E: cs-journals@wiley.co.uk

[ISSN: 0003-8504]

Prices are for six issues and include postage
and handling charges. Periodicals postage
paid at Jamaica, NY 11431. Air freight and
mailing in the USA by Publications Expediting
Services Inc, 200 Meacham Avenue, Elmont,
NY 11003.
Individual rate subscriptions must be paid by
personal cheque or credit card. Individual rate
subscriptions may not be resold or used as
library copies.

All prices are subject to change
without notice.

Postmaster
Send address changes to 3 Publications
Expediting Services, 200 Meacham Avenue,
Elmont, NY 11003

RIGHTS AND PERMISSIONS
Requests to the Publisher should be
addressed to:
Permissions Department
John Wiley & Sons Ltd
The Atrium
Southern Gate
Chichester
West Sussex PO19 8SQ
England

F: +44 (0)1243 770620
E: permreq@wiley.co.uk

CONTENTS

⚏

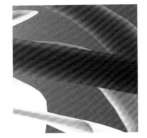

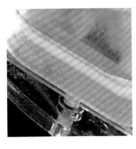

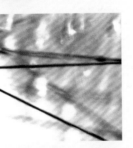

AD+

Editorial

Helen Castle

This is one of the most conspicuously provocative titles of *AD* that I have ever worked on. It immediately provokes with its alarming, gory, often carnal fleshy imagery. It is certainly not a publication for the faint-hearted. (Being one of those people who flicks channels whenever a medical procedure comes on telly, I have to admit to choosing to print out the proofs in black and white rather than colour.) The guest-editors, Marcos Cruz and Steve Pike, are certainly intending the articles in the issue to provide a wake-up call for architects and designers, and to incite debate. *Neoplasmatic Design* is not, though, about 'making waves' and shocking for shocking's sake. As they outline in their introduction, Cruz and Pike are intent on the investigation of the impact of 'emerging and progressive biological advances upon architectural and design practice'. This covers a wide range of disciplines, encompassing biology, microbiology, biotechnology, medicine and surgery. They are not dilettantes. They have both already invested a considerable amount of time in their own specialist research before coming together for this issue: with Cruz writing his doctoral thesis at the Bartlett on the 'The Inhabitable Flesh of Architecture', and Pike

collaborating with microbiologists on a series of installations/experiments. Accordingly, they carve out their own specialist areas within the issue, while also calling on the knowledge of other contributors – architects, engineers, medical authors and artists/researchers – from around the world.

Why this title is so provocative from an architectural point of view is that it puts forward a wholly new proposition for architecture. It challenges the very notion of what the substance of architecture is and what it can be: in medicine the 'neoplasm' of the title alludes literally to a tumour, but here Cruz and Pike adopt the broader definition of artists/researchers Oron Catts and Ionat Zurr, for neoplasm as a 'semi-living entity'; stretching that entity from primarily that of tissue to other bio-architectural composites. Whereas architecture as we currently know it is almost exclusively confined to dead matter – timber, brick, steel and concrete – the neoplasmatic of this *AD* is made up of emerging organisms, whether they are cultured flesh, algae or vegetation. This is not only a matter of mass, but also constitution. At its most far-reaching, the vision is one of architectonic nervous systems, organs and human hybridisation – personified by Cruz's spectre of the cyborg.

The concept of the neoplasmatic communicated in this *AD* is made all the more potent by Cruz and Pike's heady mix of projects, with no real differentiation being made between the visionary, speculative and built. For instance, it encompasses Cruz's Cyborgian In-Wall Creatures and Kol/Mac's well-developed INVERSAbrane project as well as the very real, green Wonderwall of VenhoevenCS's Sportplaza Mercator in Amsterdam. This not only suspends our sense of disbelief, but also shocks us with the realisation of what is already possible. It hastens the prospect of the neoplasmatic, placing it within our grasp. △

Marcos Cruz, Synthetic Neoplasm, 1998
Collage of human organs showing the inner side of a synthetic neoplasm. Latex imprint 2,500 x 450 mm (detail).

Neoplasmatic Design

Introduction

By Marcos Cruz and Steve Pike

The rapid development of innovative technological approaches in the realms of biology, microbiology, biotechnology, medicine and surgery are becoming of immense significance to architecture, demanding our attention due to their inevitable cultural, aesthetic and technical implications. This edition of *AD* investigates the impact of these emerging and progressive biological advances upon architectural and design practice. It presents the current groundswell of experiments and creations that utilise design as a method to explore and manipulate actual biological material.

A notion of design is emerging in which interdisciplinary work methodologies, traded between physicians, biologists and engineers, as well as artists and designers, are increasingly occurring, giving rise to hybrid technologies, new materiality and hitherto unimaginable potentially living forms. The results of these conditions, defined here as 'neoplasmatic',[1] are partly designed object and partly living material. The line between the natural and the artificial is progressively blurred. More than derived from scaled-up analogies between biological conditions (cellular structures) and larger-scale constructs (architecture), as commonly expressed in much contemporary bio-architectural work, Neoplasmatic Design implies 'semi-living'[2] entities

Design Experimentation With Bio-Architectural Composites

that require completely new definitions. In this context, the expression is to be considered a concept that is continuously developing, embracing a variety of experiments that cannot be understood as a cohesive and coherent body of work. The projects and art works featured in this issue, more than being organisms (a term historically determined by distinctly functional overtones) or assemblages (typically digitally driven geometric systems), are bio-architectural composites that, at times, appear as constructed entities or otherwise emerge rather more like living beings.

Tobias Klein (Unit 19, Bartlett School of Architecture, UCL), Syncretic Transplants, 2008
Derived from the use of non-invasive visualisation techniques in medicine, syncretic transplants are the result of a reverse-engineered process in which raw data of a human MRI scan is transformed into a three-dimensional composition of variable spatial frequencies. This creates a visceral state of fluctuation between real and virtual human flesh.

Neoplasmatism stands in the light of a phenomenon that could be referred to as the 'biologicalisation' of our world. We are constantly exposed to mainstream media coverage of biology-related themes and we encounter them continually. Terminology such as 'genetic engineering', 'cloning', 'transgenics', 'pharmaceutical design', 'plastic surgery' and 'bio-terrorism' are but a few phrases that now form the common language of our society. Yet architecture continues to be seen as fundamentally removed from such phenomena, particularly when it is understood as a discipline exclusively concerned with the built environment. Neoplasmatic Design acknowledges the considerable value of previous publications such as David Pearson's *New Organic Architecture* (2001), Günther Feuerstein's

Biomorphic Architecture (2002), Deborah Gans' and Zehra Kuz's *The Organic Approach to Architecture* (2003), Javier Senosiasin's *Bio-Architecture* (2003) and Michael Hensel, Achim Menges and Michael Weinstock's *AD*s on morphogenetic design – *Emergence* (March 2004), *Techniques and Technologies* (March 2006) and *Versatility and Vicissitude* (March 2008) – but differentiates and deviates from them. Its position is critically different; it investigates an emergent territory that explores contemporary biological practices and their implications for the field of architecture.

Biological and natural principles have been used as a model for architecture in a variety of ways. In what the Austrian architectural historian Günther Feuerstein called 'biomorphic architecture', anthropomorphic principles have long been applied to buildings, supposedly establishing a formal link between nature and architecture.[3] Le Corbusier and many of his followers, for example, suggested that a

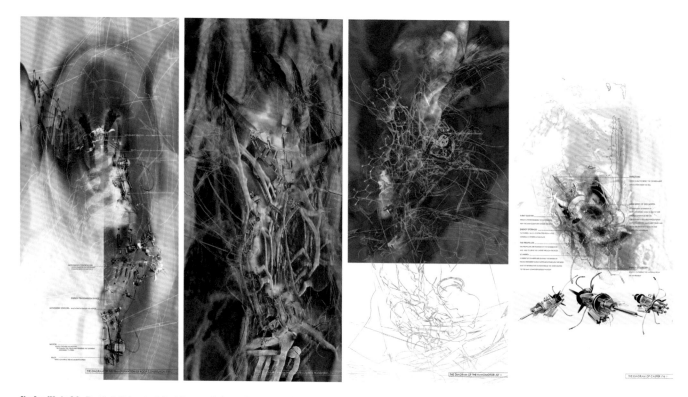

Jia Lu (Unit 20, Bartlett School of Architecture), Bone Growth Enhancement, 2001–02
The aspiration of altering the human body begins with the growth and manipulation of bone tissue inside the body. By inserting micro-machinery the natural transformation process from soft to hard tissue can be determined in terms of speed, rigidity and performance.

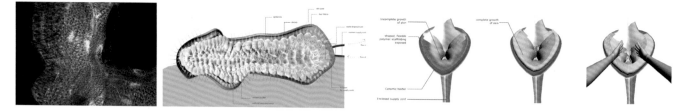

Stefanie Surjo (Unit 20, Bartlett School of Architecture), Artificial Skin, 2004–05
1) Synthetic skin created from octopus cells.
2) Cross-section through a synthetic pet grown out of human cells.
3) User diagram of a synthetic hand warmer partly constructed out of artificially grown human skin.

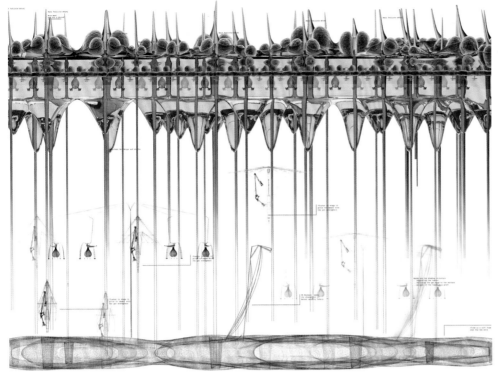

Cross-section of human skin with inserted micro-machinery used for growth enhancement, supply of nutrients and pH regulators.

Samuel White (Unit 20, Bartlett School of Architecture), Cellular Growth Enhancement, 2003–04
Views from within a Petri dish in which the growth of human skin cells – keratynocites – is enhanced with the incision of micro-machinery.

building functioned like an organism and therefore could be organised to comply with similar laws to those that regulate living systems. D'Arcy Thompson's familiar, seminal book *On Growth and Form*[4] possesses immense resonance for generations of architects. Buckminster Fuller, Frei Otto, Eero Saarinen and many besides studied biological phenomena in morphological terms and applied the principles as a means to develop new structural and formal systems.

Aside from architecture and engineering, numerous other scientific fields have engaged with biological issues, including aerodynamics, hydrodynamics, biomechanics and immunotronics. In the last field, scientists are offering new answers for artificial immune systems, attempting to apply principles found in biology to create computer hardware that can repair or evolve new functional parts when needed. Biotechnology, including disciplines such as genetics, molecular biology, biochemistry, embryology and cell biology, as well as chemical engineering, information technology and robotics, is the area in which developments possess, for better or worse, the highest potential for changing the way we understand life. A number of animal species have been cloned, the human genome has been sequenced, as has the genome of a number of other species. Furthermore, the availability of transgenic organisms

denotes a hybridising trend within biology. It is hardly surprising that so many practitioners from different fields are entering biological and medical research laboratories with the purpose of utilising the available knowledge within the realm of their own disciplines.[5] A number of artists have explored the potential aesthetic impact of employing imagery created by medical or laboratory equipment, or even utilising their own body as an instrument of art. Biology and medicine have in these cases become a new plastic medium. Plastic surgery, endoscopy, colonoscopy and echography are being used as tools for artistic expression, hence presenting a non-Cartesian approach to biology and medicine. But it is the increasing possibility of planning and designing new living conditions that is creating the biggest challenge for all implicated professions, and none more so than designers.

Perhaps most relevant for the work presented in this issue of *AD* is that which the author Kevin Kelly called 'neo-biological'. His commentary, although more than a decade old, is still important because it offers a broader picture of how our physical surroundings will become increasingly infused with 'principles of bio-logic', merging 'engineered technology and unrestrained nature until the two [will] become indistinguishable'.[6] Kelly envisaged that 'in the coming neo-biological era … there might be a world of mutating buildings, living silicon polymers, software programs evolving offline, adaptable cars, rooms stuffed with coevolutionary furniture, gnatbots for cleaning, manufactured biological viruses that cure your illnesses, neural jacks, cyborgian body parts, designer food crops, simulated personalities, and a vast ecology of computing devices in constant flux.'[7] But however

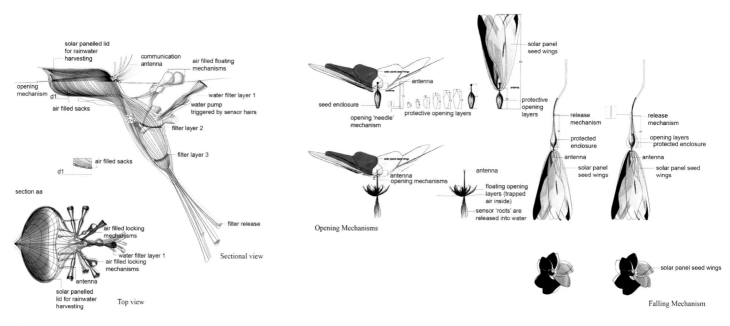

Sarracenia Aqua Sensitivus

Acer Aero Sensitivus

Minna Ala-Jaaski (Unit 20, Bartlett School of Architecture), Bio-Mechanical Hybrid Plant Species, 2007–08
These half natural, half artificial species were designed to act as biomechanical sensor mechanisms in the natural environment, detecting and responding to environmental changes such as pollution in air or water, each based on research done on a specific type of thigmonastic plant.

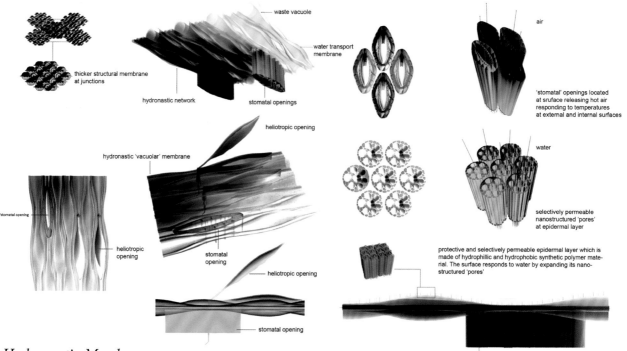

Hydronastic Membrane

Minna Ala-Jaaski, Hydronastic Membrane, 2007–08
The concept of a 'hydronastic' membrane structure is based on the function of plant cellular mechanisms of turgor pressure and the secretory, excretory and storage function role of the 'vacuole' within plant cells. In architectural design, this kind of hydromorphic membrane can be described as a hydro-biomechanical structure, which uses water and responsive polymeric materials within a series of semi-permeable membranes, acting as a filtering biosensor.

Anders Christiansen (Unit 20, Bartlett School of Architecture), Homeostasis in Architecture: Biosynthetic Ecology – An Aquatic Eco-Enhancing Implant, 2007–08
Based on the ongoing research into ocean iron fertilisation, fermentation mechanisms and algae bioreactors, the proposed artificial ecology creates a family of responsive, interrelated devices. The project is located in the urban habitat of the waterworks in east London. Here, a variety of different devices blend variable input from the surrounding natural habitat and human influences into an educational spectacle. The impact of any human interference, for example light and sound pollution from nearby roads, is recorded and processed ecologically so that it is beneficial in developing and strengthening the natural habitat.

Anders Christiansen, Homeostasis in Architecture: Floating Weather Station – Cross-Section, 2007–08
The weather station of the artificial ecology provides information from above and below the water surface to other devices. The 'tentacles' of the device reflect the movement in the water, determining changing flows of water and its biochemical balance.

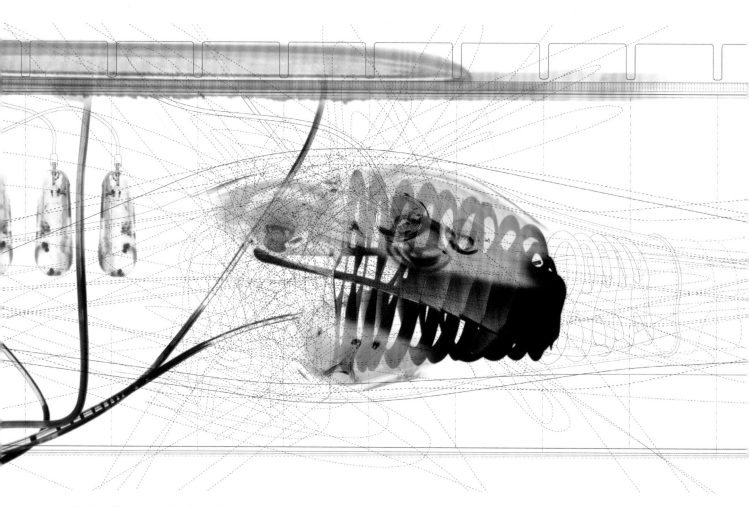

Steve Pike (Unit 20, Bartlett School of Architecture), Contaminant, 2003
Longitudinal section through Holborn Station indicating the semi-living assembly of Monitor Vessels, support infrastructure and captured microbial growth, located to interrupt and utilise the vascular network of the London Underground system.

plausible such descriptions may be, *Neoplasmatic Design* does not purport to put forward a complete vision of the future wherein architecture is fully replaced by neo-biological conditions, but rather an evolving scenario in which pre-existent, more traditional surroundings will be infiltrated by it, creating new hybrids and composite living environments. The articles and projects featured in the issue, rather than presenting predictive visions, are to be considered as provocations or wake-up calls, creating debate in architecture that goes beyond the mainstream paradigms based purely on geometrically driven discourses in the digital realm.

Ultimately, *Neoplasmatic Design* stands for the conviction that changes are occurring in architecture that demand to be understood outside the traditional disciplinary boundaries. The prophecies put forward by Kevin Kelly and Steven Levy,[8] as well as architects such as William Mitchell[9] and Neil Spiller,[10] have alerted us to the fact that architecture is undergoing profound changes and that architects are thus forced to rethink their parameters with regard to both professional practice and education: not only the manner in which we understand our body and its place within its natural habitat, but also how architects are going to respond when buildings are hybridised with biological matter, creating semi-living systems of a rather unpredictable nature. How are designers going to understand design when it implies notions of programming, control and maintenance of cellular structures that grow, evolve and eventually mutate? In the advent of such potential developments our professional practice is being critically challenged, not just in terms of the tools we may employ, our expertise and body of knowledge and emerging interdisciplinary work methodologies, but also in terms of its aesthetic intent. Are we finally capable of escaping the constraints imposed by the long-standing heritage of the aesthetics of cleanliness that affected architecture so profoundly throughout the last century, enabling us to embrace notions of dirt, impurity and ugliness as part of contemporary architectural aesthetics?

The sustainable imperative so prevalent in current architectural practice bears considerable relevance to neoplasmatic investigations, though it by no means dictates constraints. Certain living materials offer consequential benefits in terms of sustainability and may well

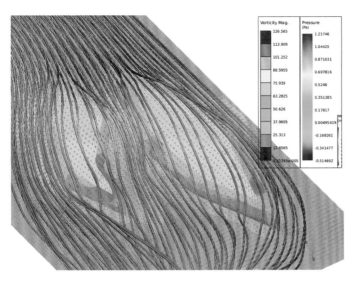

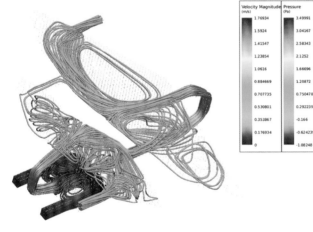

Abdur Razzak (DS10, University of Westminster), Studies of Algae Flow, 2007–08
Test of algae cultivation containers inserted in the roof of a ferry terminal in Istanbul, Turkey. CD-Adapco computer-simulation software is used to help in designing and analysing the system, and to work out a variety of different circulation patterns and flows in the algae solution.

provide commercial motivation for research and development. However, while maintaining awareness of this potential, neoplasmatic constructs are concerned with broader parameters beyond the considerations described by 'green' or 'sustainable' terminology. A more pertinent question is whether our traditional vocabulary and language is still enough to express new environments that are potentially half grown and half manufactured. New terms mainly borrowed from biological and medical sciences are already being introduced, having wide-reaching etymological implications upon architectural language. This includes the impact of 'morphogenesis',[11] 'hydronacism'[12] or 'homeostasis'[13] as terms that are changing the way in which we understand architecture. As Mitchell has astutely recognised, 'as designers tentatively embrace concepts of emergence, self-organization, self-assembly, and self-replication, they start to sound like biologists.'[14] In this context, the Tissue Culture and Art Project (TC&A) in SymbioticA continues to be crucial in testing new phenomena and elaborating new vocabulary that articulates the potential of new 'semi-living' conditions, or 'object-beings that evolve in partial life'.[15]

Relevant written and created works proliferate in the arts, particularly that considered contemporary Carnal Art, Cyber Art and, above all, Bio Art. This includes, among others, the work of Orlan (who has used numerous surgical interventions to alter her own body), Stelarc (Extra Ear – 1/4 Scale, 2003–07; Partial Head, 2005–06), Eduardo Kac (GFP Bunny, 2000; The Eighth Day, 2001; Move 36, 2002–04), the Tissue Culture and Art Project (Semi-Living Worry Dolls, 2000; Pig Wings, 2001–03; MEART, 2002–03; Semi-Living Food: 'Disembodied Cuisine', 2000–03; Victimless Leather, 2004–08), Ken Rinaldo (Augmented Fish Reality, 2004), George Gessert (Genomic Art, 2001–06), Natalie Jeremijenko (One Tree, 2000), Marta de Menezes (Nature?, 2000; Nucleart, 2003), Adam Zaretsky (Transplant Sculpting, 2001), Rachel Chapman (Breathe, 2001) and the activist, artist and Critical Art Ensemble co-founder Steve Kurtz. In addition, extensive design investigations continue to take place within a particular strain of work produced in Unit 20 at the Bartlett School of Architecture, UCL (run by Salvador Perez Arroyo and Marcos Cruz from 1999–2003, and Marcos Cruz and Marjan Colletti since 2004) and,

more recently, DS10 at the University of Westminster in London (run by Marcos Cruz and Marjan Colletti since 2006), establishing a foundation for the research put forward in this issue of *AD*. The works of Minna Ala-Jaaski, Anders Christiansen, James Foster, Haroon Iqbal, Tobias Klein, Abdur Razzak, Andy Shaw, Stefanie Surjo and Samuel White have been noteworthy here. Furthermore, important explorations have been undertaken by Anthony Dunne of the MA Design Interactions Course at the Royal College of Art in London, by Hideyuki Yamashita in the Yamashita Lab at the Nagaoka Institute of Design in Japan, as well as a broad range of scattered design ideas and projects often dismissed as too speculative or simply project-hypothesis, and therefore currently unreported in architectural publications. Neoplasmatic Design proposes to illuminate such work and extend the debate on the biologicalisation of architecture.

Within the issue, the numerous proposed bio-architectural composites have been investigated through two differing yet complementary realms: the world of botanical matter and that of animal flesh. Both differ in technological complexity, the former being technically more accessible, with the embodied ecological and environmental benefits currently explored in architectural design, while the latter is undoubtedly more contentious, especially in ethical terms. Vital issues considered are the role of design in a future increasingly affected by biotechnological advances (see Anthony Dunne, 'Design for Debate', pp 92–3) and the implications of designing new semi-living or living conditions for architecture, and how these issues are addressed and indeed engaged in the context of animal flesh (see Marcos Cruz, 'Synthetic Neoplasms', pp 36–43, and 'Cyborgian Interfaces', pp 56–9) and botanic matter (Yukihiko Sugawara, 'Uto-Purification', pp 70–1; Bill Watts and Sean Affleck, 'Living Buildings', pp 78–9; François Roche, 'Bodies Without Organs – BwO', pp 68–9; and Ton Venhoeven, 'Wonderwall', pp 80–1). Another pertinent theme considered is how to control, maintain and support living conditions (Steve Pike, 'Manipulation and Control of Micro-Organic Matter in Architecture', pp 16–23; Oron Catts and Ionat Zurr, 'Growing Semi-Living Structures', pp 30–5). The role of design in the development and integration of apparatus, equipment, monitoring vessels, support systems and prosthetics that enable growth to occur in an architectural context is of significant relevance – a task typically accomplished by engineers rather than designers (see Steve Pike, 'Algaetecture and Nonsterile', pp 70–7, and 'Contaminant', pp 24–9). Additionally, new minimal surface geometry and its seminal importance in developing a new green paradigm is explored (see Sulan Kolatan, 'Minimal Surface Geometry and the Green Paradigm', pp 62–7), as are new hybrid

Andy Shaw (Unit 20, Bartlett School of Architecture), Synthetic Gardens, 2002–03
Proposal for a synthetic garden where artificially created plants generate a biomimetic landscape of botanic lushness and exuberance.
From top to bottom: Fungal-type growth, mechanical membrane structures and flower eruptions; inside the orchestrated landscape; aqueous structural elements and flowers; integration of natural landscape and aqueous structures.

Haroon Iqbal (DS10, University of Westminster), Synthetic Photosynthesis, 2006–07
The synthetic trees developed by Dr Klaus Lackner of Columbia University, which work as enhanced CO_2 absorbers and producers, has been adopted to create synthetic lattice structures in the facade and roof of a building. The limewater-coated fabric fins absorb the CO_2 from the local atmosphere in a process akin to natural photosynthesis. This is then processed to act as a catalyst to allow algae to grow and release oxygen back into the atmosphere.

work methodologies and the use of advanced visualisation and 3-D modelling software in both medical sciences and architecture (Marcos Cruz, 'Designer Surgeons', pp 46–51). Finally, the significance of nanotechnological procedures and new biomaterials is discussed (Rachel Armstrong, 'Artificial Evolution', pp 22–5, and 'Designer Materials for Architecture', pp 86–9), along with the potential to facilitate the emergence of a new aesthetic (Peter Cook, 'Comfo-Veg Club', pp 60–1; Tobias Klein, 'Density Fields in Viscous Bodies', pp 44–5; Nicola Haines, 'Human Cloning Clinic, pp 52–5; and Neil Spiller, 'Ethics, Architecture and Little Soft Machinery', pp 94–7), to some extent defined by the reconfigured language necessary to express neoplasmatic architecture. △

Notes
1. The term 'neoplasmatic' was originally used in the context of 'Neoplasmatic Architecture', an ongoing research project that Marcos Cruz started developing for his doctoral thesis 'The Inhabitable Flesh of Architecture', undertaken at the Bartlett School of Architecture, UCL (supervisors Professor Peter Cook and Professor Jonathan Hill), between 2000 and 2007.
2. This is an expression originally used by Oron Catts and Ionat Zurr of the Tissue Culture and Art Project (TC&A). See www.tca.uwa.edu.au/extra/extra-ear.html.

3. Günther Feuerstein, *Biomorphic Architecture: Human and Animal Forms in Architecture*, Edition Axel Menges (Stuttgart and London), 2002.
4. D'Arcy W Thomson, *On Growth and Form, The Complete Revised Edition*, Dover Publications (New York), 1992 (originally published as *On Growth and Form: A New Edition* by Cambridge University Press, 1942).
5. Several publications have shown this development. These include Jill Scott, *Artists-in-labs*, 2006; Natalie Jeremijenko and Eugene Thacker, *Creative Biotechnology*, 2004; the Portuguese interdisciplinary magazine *nada*, 2003–08.
6. Kevin Kelly talks about a 'neo-biological civilization', or a 'neo-biological culture'. Kevin Kelly, *Out of Control: Biology of Machines*, Fourth Estate, 1994, p 606.
7. Ibid, p 607.
8. Steven Levy, *Artificial Life: The Quest for a New Creation*, Jonathan Cape (London), 1992.
9. William Mitchell's books *City of Bits* (1996) and *ME ++* (2003) are particularly relevant.
10. Similarly, Neil Spiller's book *Digital Dreams* (1998), the *Reflexive Architecture* issue of *AD* (2002) and, more recently, *Visionary Architecture* (2004) have been very influential.
11. See both issues of *AD* guest-edited by Michael Hensel, Achim Menges and Michael Weinstock: *Emergence: Morphogenetic Design Strategies*, Vol 74, No 3, 2004 and *Techniques and Technologies in Morphogenetic Design*, Vol 76, No 2, 2006.
12. This is a term used by Minna Ala-Jaaski in her research project 'Hydronastic Membrane' undertaken at the Bartlett School of Architecture, UCL, in 2007–08.
13. This is a term used by Anders Christiansen in his research project 'Homeostasis in Architecture' undertaken at the Bartlett School of Architecture, UCL, in 2007–08.
14. Mitchell, *ME ++: The Cyborg Self and the Networked City*, MIT Press, 2003, pp 71–2.
15. See http://www.tca.uwa.edu.au/.

Manipulation and Micro–Organic Architecture

Steve Pike looks to a future in which architects will work alongside microbiologists and mycologists, in much the same way as they now engage with a team of engineering consultants. He explains how, with the merging of the design studio and laboratory, the manipulation and control of micro-organisms themselves have to take precedence in any successful design and production process.

Control of
Matter in

Steve Pike, Nonsterile, Colonial Progression, 2001
The micro-organisms *Aspergillus fumigatus*, *Aspergillus terreus*, *Micrococcus*, *Zygomycetes rhizopus* and *Penicillium digitatum* establish colonies and negotiate territory across the growth plane of a Monitor Vessel. A distinct aesthetic emerges, morphological and phenomenological, challenging prevalent preoccupations with order and hygiene while raising notions of contamination and disgust.

The environment that surrounds us is teeming with an incredible variety of micro-organisms. As our ability to view and investigate this minuscule world develops, we are becoming increasingly aware of the importance of these organisms and the contribution they make to the circumstances in which we exist. Their microbial domain presents us with notions of form, organisation, material and composition bearing considerable relevance to the environment we inhabit. The manner in which these micro-organisms colonise their environment, how they communicate, organise and negotiate their territory, along with the mechanisms and purpose they employ, provide metaphorical parallels with human colonisation. Valuable lessons regarding symbiotic relations and sustainable systems can be drawn, while touching on morally sensitive issues of growth manipulation and behaviour control.

The precedent for architects and designers to plunder nature as a resource is firmly established. As a generator of form, a source of organisational structure or a conceptual catalyst for biomimetics, the quantity and extent of work is considerable. However, in this instance, the objective is less extrapolative. The prospect for designers to engage directly with biology, botany and mycology, to design with this living material and to explore its potential, is documented to a far lesser degree.

For the designer to utilise micro-organic material in a meaningful way, with any degree of achievable intent, it is imperative that the material may be manipulated and controlled, as for other traditionally available materials. In the capacity of coordinator, designers must engage the expertise of specialists, drawing upon a body of knowledge that they themselves cannot be expected to possess. For architects, the conventional assembly of sub-consultants will be extended to include microbiologists and mycologists alongside structural engineers and mechanical and electrical engineers. Such an interdisciplinary approach is essential for the successful creation of partially living architectural hybrids.

While at UCL, the microbiologist Professor Conrad Mullineaux[1] and his department collaborated extensively with students of the Bartlett School of Architecture, whose project themes explored the utilisation of microbial material. The design studio and laboratory merged to become one and the same, with experimentation adopting a distinct design perspective. The prevailing issue of manipulation and control of micro-organisms becomes apparent from the initial stages of this process, as its absence negates any true design intervention.

A distinction needs to be drawn between the scales at which the design manipulation is taking place, the implications and consequences of which differ considerably. The microbiological scalar separation of

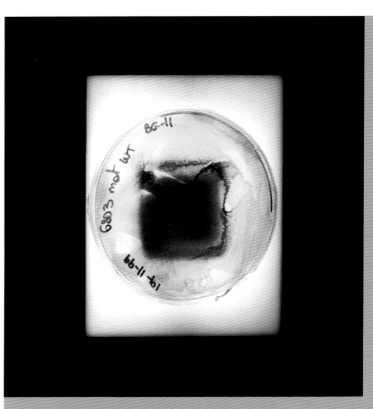

Steve Pike, Algaetecture, Cyanobacteria Manipulation, 2001
Initial investigations explored the manner in which cyanobacteria mechanisms might be manipulated. This photosensitive alga has been encouraged to grow as a square using a simple black-out mask.

nano, micro and macro scales[2] remains appropriate for designers, though as designers we rarely engage with the nano scale. Generally our traditions relate to the macro scale with only more recent, yet still atypical, forays into the smaller scales. Intervention at a subcellular level largely remains the territory of the biologist, chemical engineer or materials engineer, though in certain instances, such as genetic engineering, the intent may clearly be one of design. Micro and macro scales offer the most visually apparent potential, micro being at the cellular scale and macro embracing the broad category of everything larger. At the micro scale (cells and their accumulative colonies), design is essentially applied by controlling the environmental conditions; whereas at the macro scale, the notion may be extended to include the apparatus and infrastructure required to support the composite result.

Effective control of micro-organisms can only be achieved within closed environments; sealed vessels with filtered transmission between the interior and external conditions. All components must be sterilised and only the desired organisms must be introduced. Clearly, this is an extremely restrictive approach that limits design flexibility and which is problematic when applied to contexts beyond the laboratory. As designers, the notion of control can only be applicable by degrees, and never as an absolute. A certain amount of microbial autonomy must be embraced, manipulated by the deliberate adjustment of their

Steve Pike, Nonsterile, *Zygomycetes rhizopus*, 2001
Zygomycetes rhizopus proliferated in one Monitor Vessel, populating the vessel thoroughly and almost exclusively. In this instance, inhibitors had little effect, with the growth medium itself specifically appropriate to this microbe. The extensive colonies display complex networks of structure and communication.

immediate environment. The application or restriction of light, heat, chemical growth facilitators or inhibitors, and the provision of a tailored growth medium, all afford influence upon the proliferating microbes and their colonial progression. Particular organisms that exist in extreme environmental conditions offer the broadest scope for control; known as extremophiles,[3] they grow in specific chemical conditions, high temperatures, and high or low pH conditions where little else can survive.[4]

In order to deliver influence upon the behaviour of the living material, to partially design the result, the design and fabrication of its environment must be addressed. It is here that the hand of the designer is most apparent, in the realisation of the necessary apparatus, vessels and support structures. The aesthetic language of laboratory equipment is introduced to the vocabulary of the designer. The precise provision depends upon the integrated living material, as Mullineaux comments: 'The key thing is that you always need a water supply (either a tank of liquid, a damp surface, or a gel). Plus some way of providing appropriate raw materials for growth (light, minerals and CO_2 for a photoautotroph,[5] or an organic carbon source and perhaps oxygen for a heterotroph).[6] In most cases you

also need a way to drain or remove waste products. But this requirement can be minimised by using microbial systems; two or more different sorts of microbes feeding off each other's waste products.'[7]

The work of Yiannis Kanakakis directly addresses the design of apparatus and embraces the laboratorial language. His research undertaken at the Bartlett School of Architecture proposes a series of devices to be located in the vicinity of Liverpool Street in central London. Exploiting and channelling the rejected heat and humidity from the Underground station, the installed equipment is provided with the conditions to facilitate the capture and incubation of localised fungi. Organic data is gathered, monitoring urban activity and movement.[8]

The amalgamation of inert constructed fabric and responsive living material presents an opportunity to harness the beneficial inherent mechanisms of micro-organisms, dependent upon the specific microbe employed. For example, the relationship between humans and algae is based upon one of the most fundamental cycles of the earth's ecosystem. Algae are essentially photosynthetic organisms; similar to plants in this respect, they convert CO_2 into energy-abundant sugars, releasing oxygen as a waste product. In common with the majority of animals, humans convert oxygen to CO_2 via our respiratory process. We are intrinsically linked in a delicate gaseous balancing act. Less familiar is the potential for the absorption or deactivation of toxins, essentially the process that occurs in sewage plants. In addition,

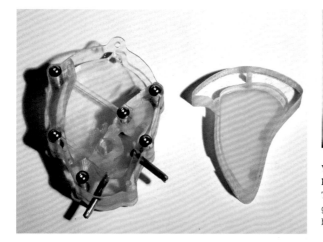

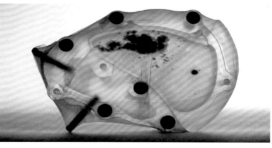

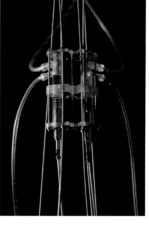

Yiannis Kanakakis (Unit 5, Bartlett School of Architecture, UCL),
Monitor Capsule, Liverpool Street Station, London, 2003
The sterilised Monitor Capsule and its associated housing. Once filled with an appropriate growth medium, the capsule is incorporated within the apparatus for exposure, before being wrapped and incubated in order to develop resultant growth.

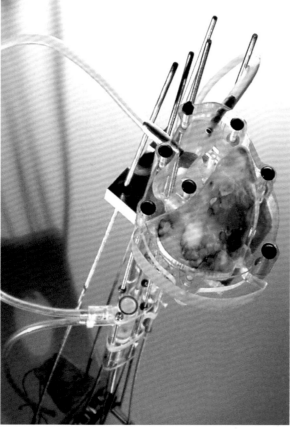

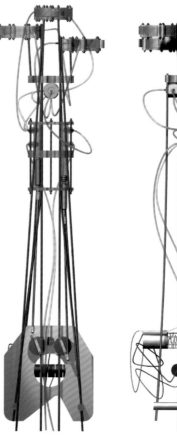

Yiannis Kanakakis,
Monitoring Apparatus,
Liverpool Street Station,
London, 2003
The assembled device collects fungi from the drainage system in and around Liverpool Street Station in London. Mechanical components such as pumps, valves and capillary systems draw the ambient organisms across Monitor Capsules installed at the top of the device, exposing the contained growth medium.

recent speculation suggests harvesting micro-organic materials or their waste products for the production of food, medicine and fuel. Though the exploration of the prospective value of such organisms is only at a preliminary stage, it is perhaps these rewards that present architectural research with the most practical benefit.

For designers to work successfully with micro-organic material, the problematic issues of scale and time must be addressed. By definition, microbes are extremely small, largely anonymous to human perception. Yet collectively their colonial progression can be substantial and therefore visibly apparent, as demonstrated by fungal decomposition, biofilms or microbial blooms. Occasionally, microbial activity employs localised inert material; such is the case with stromatolites.[9] The temporal development of microbes is similarly challenging from a designer's perspective, their growth rate generally imperceptible, though Mullineaux contests this:

For example, if you seed a liquid broth culture with a few *E.coli*, it will be cloudy within a few hours. On a microscopic scale things can be quite frenetic. We have been working with mixed cultures containing motile filamentous cyanobacteria and smaller flagellated bacteria. The cyano's glide around rather rapidly on the agar surface (like tiny worms), the flagellated bacteria swim around frantically in the liquid above. Phototaxis[10] provides one way to translate some of this action to larger scales; photosynthetic microbes will glide or swim in response to light. Because they are pigmented, you can see where they are concentrated. Over a period of a few minutes to a few hours you can get visible changes in distribution. It is possible to manipulate this behaviour genetically; there are mutants with altered phototactic behaviour.[11]

By targeting specific micro-organisms and providing the optimum environmental conditions, the issues of scale and rate of growth may be overcome to a degree. Modification at a subcellular level promises significant enhancement, though socially genetic engineering unremittingly proves contentious.

The work of Aniko Meszaros and Sean Hanna confronts the design issues of scale and time through their winning competition entry Territories of Interwoven Genetic Design. They propose the generation of a living landmass composed of genetically designed organisms; utilising the tools of biotechnology for an architectural purpose. An automated laboratory engineers 'macrophytes'[12] (specifically macro-cellular organisms derived from cyanobacteria and algae) and combines them with selected plant DNA to produce original pre-programmed species. A floating pressurised cable network provides the infrastructure by which the living material colonises the Venetian Lagoon, resulting in cyclical autogenic reproduction. As the filamentous, woven growth takes hold, designed intervention gives way to the autonomous development of an inhabitable landmass.[13]

If only partial control of the living material can realistically be achieved, then the capability to monitor is vital. To observe the progression of growth within the composite construct and to react with

Aniko Meszaros and Sean Hanna, Territories of Interwoven Genetic Design: A Living, Artificial Landscape, Venetian Lagoon, Italy, 1999
Situated in the Venetian Lagoon, a vast botanical textile is encouraged to occupy the surface of the city's polluted, unused industrial harbour. Interweaving plant with machine, organic life with urban life; a new hybrid territory is created.

the delivery of facilitators or inhibitors to influence the result is critical to avoid unrestrained microbial activity. Recent developments in microbiological practice have advanced the means to gather morphometrical[14] data. Advancements in optical technologies and interdisciplinary collaboration with physicists and mathematicians have led to specific progress in the field of systems biology and cell biology of micro-organisms – Mullineaux's specialism. An automated support system can be readily linked to a monitoring sensor, as Mullineaux explains: 'In general, microbial growth in liquid cultures can be monitored by measuring the turbidity of the liquid. This can be automated quite easily, you just need to shine a thin beam of light through the liquid with a detector on the other side. Chemostats[15] work in this way; providing the automated control of the supply of fresh medium and draining of waste culture.'[16]

The creation of partially living architectural constructs proffers the opportunity to exploit natural systems, to engage the subtle and immediate responsivity of natural dynamic mechanisms that artificially manufactured systems almost universally lack. Extrapolation of natural systematic process for the purpose of man-made interpretations remains among the most valuable and important contemporary architectural investigations.[17] However, this abstraction does not engage or incorporate living organisms directly, avoiding the degree of unpredictability that such living material introduces while renouncing many benefits. Designing with micro-organic matter demands an alternative approach in which the inevitable merging of disciplinary boundaries and responsibilities, in conjunction with the integration of the self-organisational processes of living organisms, dictates the relinquishing of absolute control on behalf of the designer. Moreover, it reveals the contaminated reality of our environment, brazenly displaying its consequential aesthetic.

To accept this visual manifestation challenges the firmly established 'aesthetic of hygiene and cleanliness', as described by Adrian Forty,[18] so deeply rooted in the visual language of our society. An assumed correlation between ordered, controlled, visually purified architectural space and hygienic conditions and good health is accepted as truth. Born of the social and medical reforms of the 19th century, the notion was enthusiastically adopted by the Modern Movement, ensuring its importance as a consideration of architectural design. The incorporation of living material in design practice and the creation of partially living architectural hybrids require a significant ideological shift; an embracing of a distinctly phenomenological aesthetic that confronts the prevalent white-walled sterility of the Modernist legacy. ∆

Aniko Meszaros and Sean Hanna, Territories of Interwoven Genetic Design: A Living, Artificial Landscape, Venetian Lagoon, Italy, 1999
The amalgamated organism evolves through biotechnology; an automated laboratory is its generator. It collects pre-existing vegetation, and genetically modifies and reconfigures it to create new growth-accelerated, responsive species that can float, support human weight, repair themselves, flower when touched, and trace the movements of fish with bioluminescence as they populate their regenerated environment.

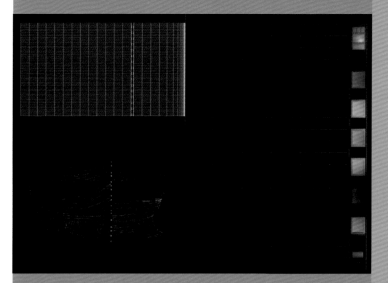

A pressurised, hollow-core cable and fibre-optic network serves as the infrastructure for planting and maintenance. This runs from the central automated lab-spine to the shores. Seeds and spores are extracted, manipulated in the laboratory, and redistributed according to data generated from field sensors.

Notes

1. The text of this article was produced following written and spoken communication with Professor Conrad Mullineaux, and was informed extensively by the process. Formerly of the Department of Microbiology at UCL, Mullineaux currently holds the position of Professor of Microbiology, specialising in photosynthesis and membrane dynamics in bacteria, at Queen Mary, University of London.

2. As Mullineaux states, by way of clarification: 'In terms of microbiology, nano means the subcellular scale (proteins and other bits of molecular machinery within the cell), micro is the cellular scale (cells and small assemblages of cells) and macro is anything bigger.' Communication with the author, 2008.

3. 'Extremophiles: An organism that requires an extreme environment in which to flourish, such as "thermophiles" existing in temperatures of up to sixty degrees Celsius, "hyperthermophiles" existing occasionally above one hundred degrees Celsius or "halophiles" that require extreme saline conditions.' In John Lackie, *The Dictionary of Cell and Molecular Biology*, Academic Press, 2007.

4. Transcribed from correspondence with the author, 2008.

5. 'Photoautotroph: Organisms that synthesise all their organic molecules from inorganic materials, light being their source of energy.' From *The Dictionary of Cell and Molecular Biology*, op cit.

6. 'Heterotroph: An organism that requires carbon compounds from other plant or animal sources and that cannot synthesise them itself'. From ibid.

7. As explained by Mullineaux in correspondence with the author, 2008.

8. Design project and research developed by Yiannis Kanakakis at the Bartlett School of Architecture, UCL, 2002–03. As part of Unit 5, this was supported by tutors Marjan Colletti and Julia Backhaus, and additionally by the Department of Microbiology, UCL.

9. As Mullineaux explains: 'Stromatolites – these are large columns formed in shallow water from sediments trapped by biofilms of photosynthetic bacteria.' Correspondence with the author, 2008.

10. 'Phototaxis: The movement of a cell or organism towards or away from a source of light.' *The Dictionary of Cell and Molecular Biology*, op cit.

11. As described by Mullineaux during correspondence with the author, 2008.

12. Macrophytes are a member of the macroscopic plant life of an area, especially of a body of water; large aquatic plants, visible with the naked eye.

13. Territories of Interwoven Genetic Design: A Living, Artificial Landscape, a Japanese Design Foundation Competition Gold Prize winner in 1999, was based on Meszaros' work Plant Anima, which was developed during the MArch in Architectural Design at the Bartlett School of Architecture, UCL, 1998/99. It was supported by Yael Reisner and Peter Cook, as well as the Department of Molecular Biology at UCL.

14. Morphometrics is the process of measuring the external shape and dimensions of living organisms.

15. 'Chemostats: Apparatus for maintaining a bacterial population in the exponential phase of growth by regulating the input of rate-limiting nutrients and the removal of medium and cells.' *The Dictionary of Cell and Molecular Biology*, op cit.

16. As explained by Mullineaux during correspondence with the author, 2008.

17. An extensive body of valuable work exists in this realm of architectural research. Among the most rigorous and important are the contemporary investigations of the Emergence and Design Group: Michael Hensel, Achim Menges and Michael Weinstock.

18. For the complete text of Forty's commentary, see Chapter 7 'Hygiene and Cleanliness' of his *Objects of Desire: Design and Society since 1750*, Thames & Hudson, 1986, p 156.

The propositional timeframe for the establishment of the hybrid landscape. From top: the initial network, after one year's development, after three years, after five years, and completely established after fifteen years.

Contaminant

Steve Pike, Contaminant, 2003
In this installation composed of steel,
glass, acrylic and micro-organisms,
visitors introduce arbitrary ambient
microbes, instigating growth across the
vertical field of Monitor Vessels.

For Contaminant, **Steve Pike** designed and crafted a structure of Monitor Cells and Monitor Vessels that set out 'to apprehend and develop locally present microbes'. Proving to be a significant investigation into the monitoring capability and responsiveness of the structure, the installation also exemplified an emergent, morphological aesthetic.

The Contaminant[1] project collectively describes a series of investigative studies culminating in a responsive architectural installation. Rather than considering the ability of micro-organisms to modify their immediate environment, as with previous work such as Algaetecture and Nonsterile, the objective of this study was to investigate the monitoring capabilities of an installation deliberately designed to apprehend and develop locally present microbes and to reveal the resultant morphological aesthetic.

Initially, a series of portable Monitor Cells was created, and exposed to particular locations and their attendant microbes in order to discover the common micro-organisms present and to identify those specific to a given environment. The results were demonstrative. *Aspergillus*, commonly present in the fabric of our built environment, and *Micrococcus* which populates the surface of our skin, proliferated across all of the Monitor Cells. But other, more distinct, microbes, directly associated with plant, fruit, bread or dairy material present at the particular site of exposure gave rise to unique visual transformations, in turn revealing an almost epidemiological history.

top: CAD/CAM production of the Monitor Cells. As a derivative of laboratory apparatus, the functional form of the Monitor Cell was initially developed by a CAD process, allowing accurate manufacturing moulds to be established. This data was then translated to enable tool path programming. The four-part moulds were then modelled with a CAM process, utilising a CNC mill, before assembly. The composite mould was employed to vacuum-form transparent acrylic sheet in order to produce multiple Monitor Cells, each possessing the precision necessary for the device to facilitate airtightness subsequent to exposure.

bottom: Preparation of the Monitor Vessels in the laboratory. Monitor Vessel plates were prepared under sterile conditions in the UCL Department of Microbiology laboratory. The potato dextrose and agar, or BG11 and agar, solutions possess specifically tailored compositions dependent upon the group of micro-organisms targeted for capture. Following heating to high temperature in an autoclave, the growth medium is applied within the sterile environment of a laminar flow extractor hood before being placed in an illuminated incubator prior to exposure.

Visitors to the installation introduce particulate matter, catalysts for the transformation of Monitor Vessels. The micro-organisms *Aspergillus fumigatus* and *Aspergillus terreus*, present in our built environment, and *Micrococcus*, found on the surface of human skin, compete for colonial territory across the growth plates. Structure, facilitators, inhibitors, moisture extracts and photo sources support the flourishing growth, composing a semi-living hybrid – an abstraction of the proposed subterranean intervention.

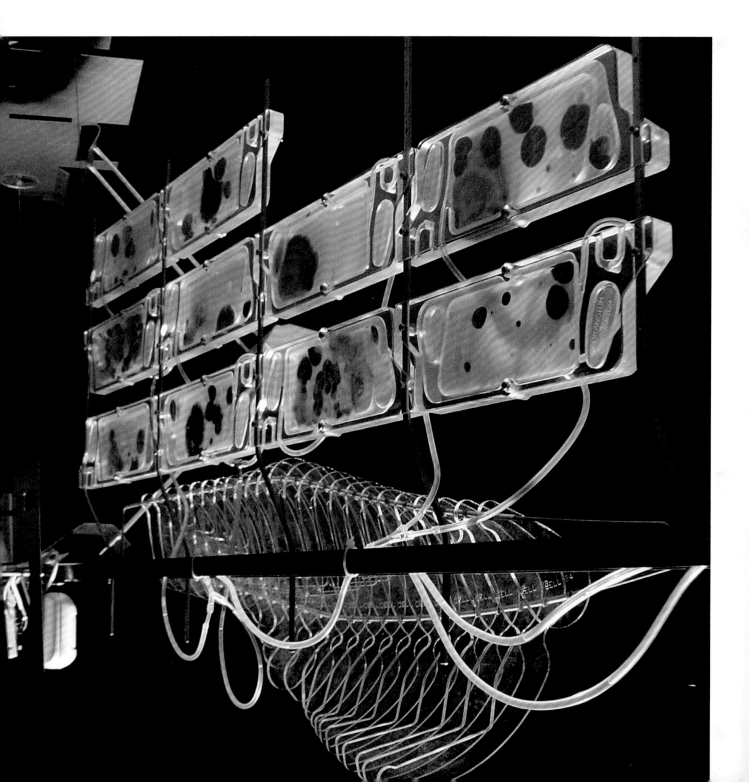

...g exposure, the developed Monitor Cells ...distinctly site-specific colonial growth. Location ...sure (clockwise, from top left): Dwelling, building site, flower market, bakery, airport.

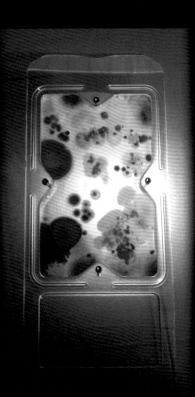
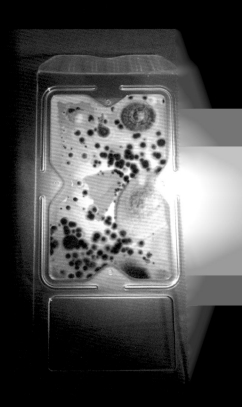
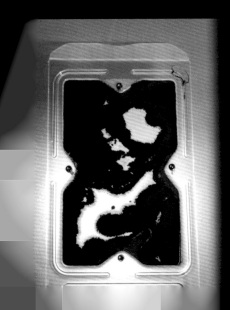
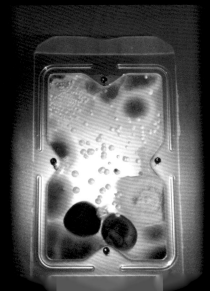

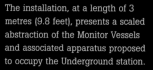

The installation, at a length of 3 metres (9.8 feet), presents a scaled abstraction of the Monitor Vessels and associated apparatus proposed to occupy the Underground station.

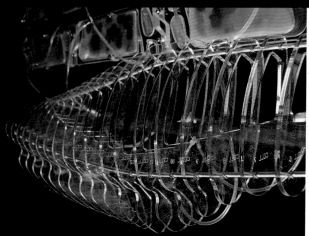

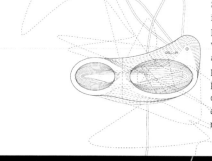

Sequential progressions. The installation incorporates a series of sequential progressions, spatial interruptions producing vascular volumes responding to potential airflow. Their form is derived from spatial progressions, a sequence of sectional parameters in which a string of non-uniform data points advance at regular incremental amounts, sequentially arranged, giving rise to non-Euclidean volumetric form.

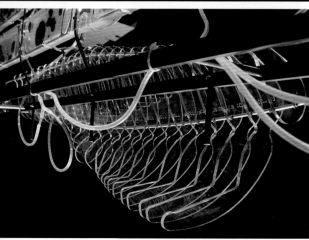

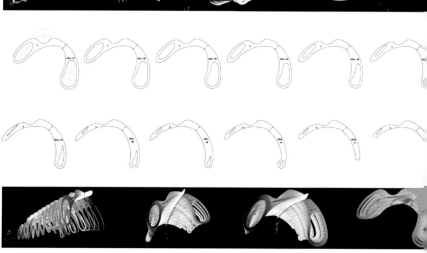

Illustrating those Monitor Vessels placed adjacent to the curved interior of the Holborn Underground Station platform, the resultant growth presents a morphological aesthetic reliant on colonial progression.

The investigation progressed to the proposition of an architectural intervention: a designed object embracing the disciplines of microbiology and mycology alongside architecture and engineering. The structure, incorporating responsive Monitor Vessels and the support systems required to sustain them, is hypothetically located where arbitrary micro-organic material would be incidentally introduced. The subterranean vascular network of the London Underground provides airborne highways for particulate matter across the city. London's inhabitants act as unwitting hosts to microbial populations, introducing catalytic material describing individual daily activity. A series of Monitor Vessels and occupational clusters was proposed to colonise a redundant portion of Holborn Underground Station, capturing and propagating the ambient particles.

To construct this proposed condition, a 1:10 scaled and abstracted installation was created, but incorporating authentic Monitor Vessels and their associated support systems to facilitate the chemical, humidity and temperature controls necessary. An architecture of contamination resulted, the fabric and spatial possibilities of the installation reconfigured with every microbial progression. ⌂

Note

1. The research, development and creation of Contaminant necessitated a distinct interdisciplinary process. As tutors of Unit 20 at the Bartlett School of Architecture, UCL, Marcos Cruz and Salvador Perez Arroyo lent indispensable design input and discourse. Professor Conrad Mullineaux and his staff at the Department of Microbiology laboratories, UCL, provided expertise, considerable assistance and facilities. Dr Richard Strange of the UCL Department of Mycology offered his expert knowledge. Abi Abdolwahabi and Bim Burton at the Bartlett workshop provided considerable technical assistance. Nick Callicott lent notable CAD/CAM support and expertise. London Underground and the staff at Holborn Station offered guidance and explanation regarding the technical logistics of the Underground system and the proposed site. Contaminant was exposed in both London and Berlin; the installation displayed differing resultant colonisations, revealing the distinct environmental conditions and suggesting the preceding activity and behaviour of the visiting public.

Growing Semi-Living Structures

Concepts and Practices for the Use of Tissue

Technologies for Non-Medical Purposes

For over a decade, artist/researchers **Oron Catts and Ionat Zurr** have led the Tissue Culture and Art Project (TC&A), hosted in SymbioticA – The Centre of Excellence in Biological Arts, the School of Anatomy and Human Biology at the University of Western Australia. It has provided a unique context for their explorations, enabling them to pioneer new ways of growing tissue for artistic purposes outside the ethical strictures of medical laboratories, while also subverting and questioning scientific tools and techniques.

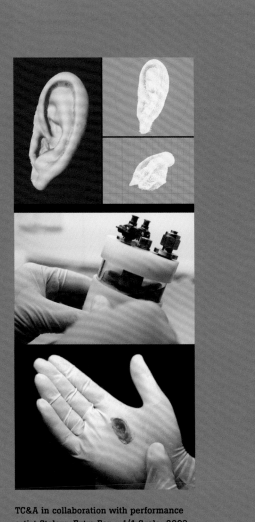

TC&A in collaboration with performance artist Stelarc, Extra Ear – 1/4 Scale, 2003
top: Visualised data from a three-dimensional scan of Stelarc's left ear.
centre: The ear in a bioreactor.
bottom: The fully grown ear.
opposite: Medium: Biodegradable polymer and human chondrocytes cells. Dimensions of original: 3.0 x 1.5 x 1.5 cm.

The body is becoming a regenerative site while at the same time it disintegrates; such is the promise of body parts regrowing in and out of bodies. In this world, parts of bodies are being grown outside their original context in different configurations. Some cells have been grown continuously outside their original body for more than 60 years.[1] The realisation that cells from complex organisms can not only be sustained alive outside the body, but can also grow, divide and function came in the 1910s when Dr Alexis Carroll began his experiments in a technique he called 'tissue culture'. However, it was another 80 years before it was realised that cells can be grown in three dimensions to form a functional tissue that has the potential to replace missing or failing body parts. This development came from the collaborative work of surgeon Dr Joseph Vacanti, and a material scientist, Dr Robert Langer, who developed a system that uses specially designed degradable polymers that act as a scaffold for the developing tissue.[2]

A layer of pig mesenchymal cells (bone-marrow stem cells) grown for six weeks as part of Oron Catts' and Ionat Zurr's residency as research fellows at the Tissue Engineering and Organ Fabrication Laboratory, Massachusetts General Hospital, Harvard Medical School, 2001.

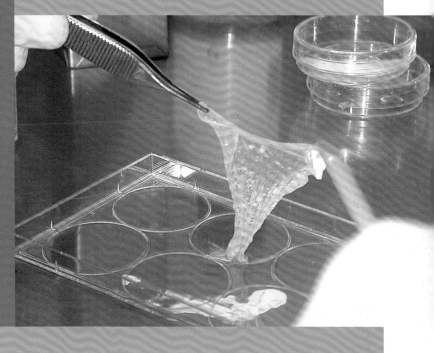

Fifteen years after Vacanti and Langer coined the term 'tissue engineering', which 'applies the principles of biology and engineering to the development of functional substitutes for damaged tissue',[3] the growth of three-dimensional 'functional' tissues is no longer confined to the biomedical world. As other aspects of regenerative medicine such as stem cell therapy, therapeutic cloning and cell engineering are increasingly dominating the field, technologies that were originally developed for tissue engineering in the 1990s are now used for non-clinical ends. Tissues and cells from complex organisms are grown in large quantities for the production of biological substances; liver cells are being grown as toxicity sensors; different cells from different sources (bodies and organs) are grown together in micro-fluidic chambers to make 'animals' on chips as an alternative to animal and human drug testing; in-vitro meat is seriously considered as an alternative to traditional meat production; and an increasing number of artists, designers and architects are working with living tissues as part of their practice.

The Tissue Culture and Art Project (TC&A) was set up in 1996 to explore, develop and critique the use of tissue technologies for artistic ends. The project focuses mainly on investigating human relationships with the different gradients of life through the construction/growth of a new class of object/being – that of the 'semi-living'. These are parts of complex organisms that are sustained alive outside the body and coerced to grow in predetermined shapes. Evocative objects, they are a tangible example that brings into question deep-rooted perceptions of life and identity, the concept of self, and the position of the

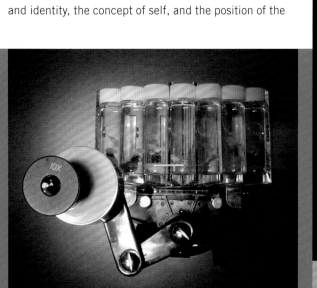

TC&A, Semi-Living Worry Dolls, 2000
Semi-Living Worry Dolls display. Medium: Cells, biodegradable/bioabsorbable polymers and surgical sutures. Dimensions of original: variable.

TC&A, Pig Wings, 2000–01
From top to bottom: The chiropteran version. Medium: Pig mesenchymal cells (bone-marrow stem cells) and biodegradable/bioabsorbable polymers (PGA, P4HB). Dimensions of original: 4.0 x 2.0 x 0.5 cm each; CAD drawing of a chiropteran wing made by Oron Catts through observations of the specimen at the Harvard University Museum; Pig mesenchymal cells (bone-marrow stem cells) grown over/into biodegradable/bioabsorbable polymers (PGA, P4HB). The construct was grown for eight months in a microgravity bioreactor. Dimensions of original: 4.0 x 2.0 x 0.5 cm each.

Left: Biodegradable/bioabsorbable polymer (PGA, P4HB) constructs are seeded with cells and nutrient media inside a bioreactor vessel.
Centre: Pig wing tissue constructs are being 'fed' with nutrient media. Right: Oron Catts and a surgeon colleague harvesting bone-marrow stem cells.

human in regard to other living beings and the environment. Particularly interested in the new discourses and new ethics, epistemologies and ontology that surround issues of partial life and the contestable future scenarios they are offering us, TC&A has thus researched and developed new ways of growing tissue, using and subverting scientific tools and techniques dating from almost a hundred years ago to the present.

A New Body

Eduard Uhlenhuth wrote in 1916: 'Through the discovery of tissue culture we have, so to speak, created a new type of body on which to grow the cell.'[4] In order to be able to grow these tissue cells outside bodies in-vitro (in glass), it was necessary to engineer a new kind of 'body', one that would provide at least the minimum necessary conditions for the cells to act as they would in a living body. This included the right nutrients and temperature, and a substrate on which cells that needed anchoring could grow. But, above all, the cells needed a sterile environment, a system that separated them from the rest of the living and hostile world – a spaceship of sorts.

As demands from the tissues (in function, form and complexity) have increased, new techno-scientific bodies (or 'epibodies') have been developed. These devices/bodies are commonly known as 'bioreactors', a term that to an extent confirms the instrumentalisation of living fragments and alludes to the tissues' new role as means of production. Some bioreactors go beyond the minimal body conditions outlined above and provide other mechanical and environmental applications such as pulsation (for the growth of blood vessels), mechanical stress (for the formation of muscle fibres), and timed release of growth and differentiation factors.

The main obstacle in growing tissue constructs in three dimensions is that of plumbing. Growing large constructs (more than approximately 10 layers of cells – 200 microns) is difficult due to the lack of nutrient solution delivery; thus constructing or growing an artificial capillary system in such a resolution has not yet been achieved. Though there are ways of providing mass transport of nutrients, these can be analogous to primitive irrigation techniques, and though they allow for relatively thick growth in bioreactors (up to about 4 millimetres/0.16 inches), tissue that grows this way cannot be perfused or implanted in the body.

Biology, Engineering and the Semi-Living

HG Wells, writing a short journalistic meditation called 'The Limits to Individual Plasticity' in the London *Saturday Review* in 1895, made a case for the plasticity of the body. He wrote: 'We overlook only too often the fact that a living being may also be regarded as raw material, as something plastic, something that may be shaped and altered.'[5]

Almost a hundred years later, Ezio Manzini pondered 'what are the anthropological implications of the widespread penetration of technological science on the products of our daily lives?' He then offered the following scenario:

> think of objects not as instruments for our use, but as entities that are effectively linked and that need care – think of objects as plants in our garden ... Think of objects that are beautiful and useful as trees in your own garden, objects that endure and have lives of their own, objects that perform services and, require care ... I am thinking of criteria of quality that lead to a system of objects that have the variety, complexity, life and blend of beauty and utility of a garden but, at the same time, are a product of the real world, a world extensively and intensively artificial.[6]

Combining these two ways of thinking about our made and grown world in the context of tissue engineering, in 1996 Oron Catts asked: 'If we can grow something as complex as an organ outside of the body why re-implant them back into the body? If we can grow and sustain alive for long periods of time something as complex as an organ why stay loyal to the original design? If this is possible why not grow/construct tools for our use? And if this is possible, there is still the major question should we go down this path?'[7]

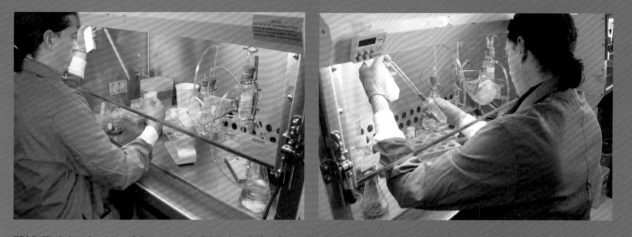

TC&A, Victimless Leather – A Prototype of a Stitch-less Jacket Grown in a Technoscientific 'Body', 2004
Assembly of the Victimless Leather perfusion system and seeding of the polymer jacket in sterile conditions.

This question led to a succession of artistic research projects that included Semi-Living Worry Dolls (2000), Pig Wings (2000–01), Extra Ear – 1/4 Scale (2003), and a series of works that dealt, with much irony, with the 'technologically mediated victimless utopia' that involved the creation of tissue-engineered in-vitro meat and leather in projects such as Semi-Living Food: 'Disembodied Cuisine' (2003) and Victimless Leather (2004–08). All of these projects used similar processes of constructing three-dimensional polymer scaffolds in the desired shape, seeding them with the appropriate cells and growing them in specialised bioreactors. Some of the three-dimensional forms were achieved by using CAD/CAM (such as the 1/4 scale ear and the pig wings), while others were handcrafted or cut to shape from sheets of polymer mesh.

In order to display TC&A's living tissue-engineered constructs, or 'semi-living sculptures', it was sometimes necessary to design and build site-specific laboratories in galleries. Bioreactors were even designed to deal with the special requirements of showing semi-living sculptures in an artistic context.

The intention is not to provide yet another consumer product, but rather to raise questions about the exploitation of other living beings. The role of the artist is to provide symbolic yet tangible examples of possible futures, and research the potential effects of these new forms on our cultural perceptions of life. It is not the artist's role to provide people with goods for their daily use. The emphasis is on seeing the work in a cultural rather than a commercial context.

One role of art is to suggest scenarios of 'worlds under construction' and subvert technologies for the purpose of creating contestable objects. It is this role that makes the emergence of the semi-living as evocative art 'objects', and the multi-levelled exploration of their use, so relevant. ∆

Medium: Biodegradable polymer connective and bone cells. Dimensions of original: variable.

TC&A, Semi Living Food: 'Disembodied Cuisine', 2003
Installation at the 'L'art Biotech' exhibition in Nantes, France.

Notes

1. NCTC clone 929 (Connective tissue, mouse) Clone of strain L was derived in March 1948. Strain L was one of the first cell strains to be established in continuous culture, and clone 929 was the first cloned strain to be developed. The parent L strain was derived from normal subcutaneous areolar and adipose tissue of a 100-day-old male C3H/An mouse. See http://www.atcc.org/ATCCAdvancedCatalogSearch/ProductDetails/tabid /452/Default.aspx?ATCCNum=CCL-1&Template=cellBiology.
2. R Langer and JP Vacanti, 'Tissue Engineering', in *Science*, Vol 260, Issue 5110, 14 May 1993, pp 920–26.
3. Ibid.
4. Eduard Uhlenhuth, 'Changes in pigment epithelium cells and iris pigment cells of rana pipiens induced by changes in environmental conditions', *Journal of Experimental Medicine*, 24:689–699, 1916, p 690.
5. HG Wells, 'The limits of individual plasticity', in RM Philmus and DY Hughes (eds), *H. G. Wells: Early Writings in Science and Science Fiction*, University of California Press (Berkeley, CA), 1975, p 36.
6. Ezio Manzini and John Cullars, 'Prometheus of the Everyday: The Ecology of the Artificial and the Designer's Responsibility', in *Design Issues*, Vol 9, No 1, Autumn 1992, pp 5–20.
7. Oron Catts, 'Custom Grown Organic Surface Coating', Honours Thesis, Curtin University of Technology, Western Australia, 1996.

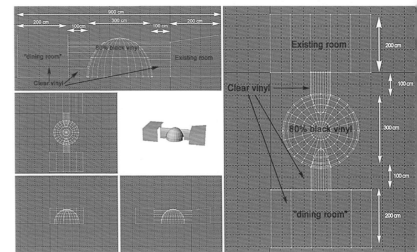

CAD drawings of a site-specific laboratory designed by the artists for the installation in Nantes.

Synthetic
Neoplasms

Marcos Cruz explores the cultural precedents for the evolution of synthetic neoplasms – artificial matter and bio-synthetic flesh composites. He draws on a rich artistic and filmic lineage, ranging from the hybrid forms of 16th-century Breugel to Patricia Piccinini's more recent mutant creations, and most vividly and perhaps alarmingly the flesh formations of the game-pods in David Cronenberg's 1999 film *eXistenZ*.

Marcos Cruz, *Synthetic Neoplasm*, 1998
Collage of human organs showing the inner side of a synthetic neoplasm.

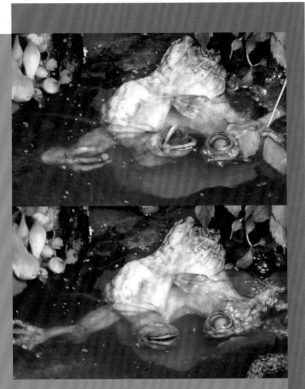

David Cronenberg, *eXistenZ*, 1999
A mutated amphibian derived from fertilised eggs infused with synthetic DNA lying in water before being mutilated and surgically reassembled into a game-pod.

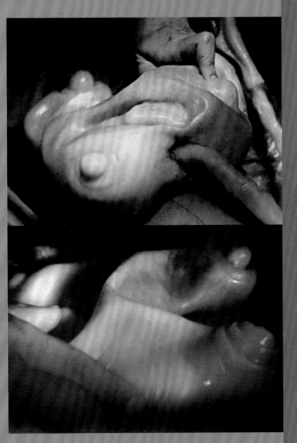

Touching the game-pod resembles an act of kneading.

The material and functional hybridisation of biological and non-biological systems has been explored in an increasingly diverse manner in art and film, having its most extreme expression in a series of animal-like objects that are still difficult to classify. This is due to their formal and material character, the complexion of their skin, as well as their status as 'object-beings'[1] and the manner in which these establish a new relationship with the human body. David Cronenberg's movie *eXistenZ* (1999)[2] and the weird game-pods featured in it are a pivotal example of such hybridisation, requiring a more careful examination.

The film revolves around an ambiguous real/virtual experience in which players of a game called *eXistenZ* connect themselves to pods that become physically plugged into their nervous system. Although referred to in the movie as creatures, it is not clear what the pods in actual fact are. Should they be considered as kinds of mutants or chimeras that share partly robotic, partly human features, calling to mind old mythologies of Cyclopes or aliens? Or should they simply be understood in terms of what Greg Lynn has defined as 'blobs'?

In a first analysis, Cronenberg's game-pods have a topological complexity that is akin to Lynn's blobs. But more than geometrically driven 'proto-objects',[3] which are digitally generated from scaled-up analogies between biology and architecture, they are in fact biological formations that lack a clear and recognisable geometry. They seem to share features with what the French philosopher George Bataille considered '*informe*'; a sense of carnal 'horizontality', the use of a 'base materialism' of flesh that has a formless and even scatological dimension, the emergence of an internal biological 'pulse', and a potential to become entropic,[4] as opposed to Lynn's generative and constructive blob models.[5] On the whole, Cronenberg's game-pods possess a unique materiality due to their 'semi-living'[6] status, suggesting that they are neoplasms[7] instead.

Detail view of a game-pod with an inlucent skin.

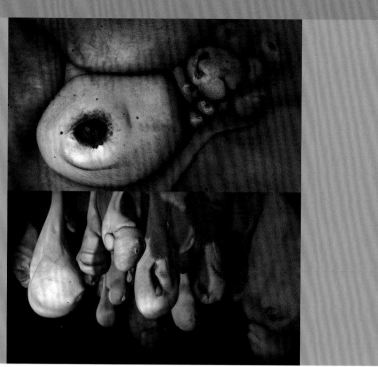

above:
Patricia Piccinini, *Still Life with Stem Cells*, 2002
Silicone, polyurethane, human hair, clothing and carpet. Life-size,
dimensions variable.
top right:
Patricia Piccinini, *Plasmid Region*, 2003
DVD, 16:9 PAL with sound; 20-minute loop.
bottom right:
Patricia Piccinini, *In Bocca Al Lupo*, 2003
DVD, 16:9 PAL with sound; 20-minute loop.

The term 'neoplasm' is borrowed from medicine where it stands for what in common language is called a tumour. Its medical definition describes it as 'a mass of abnormal tissue that arises without obvious cause from pre-existing body cells, has no purposeful function, and is characterized by a tendency to independent and unrestrained growth'.[8] In Cronenberg's film, however, more than it being understood as a pathological occurrence it refers to the formal quality of being 'plasmatic';[9] that is, a strange-looking lump of autonomous flesh that proves to be somehow alive. Such characteristics are clearly not exclusive to Cronenberg's propositions, and are also evident in the extraordinary and prolific artwork of Patricia Piccinini who creates a variety of mutant and hybrid organisms of an unprecedented formal character.

The product design of Droog/Frank Tjepkema, as well as architectural proposals by Samuel White, Stefanie Surjo and Tobias Klein also express such plasmatic features. Since these neoplasms are all artificially created and not grown out of the human body, it makes sense to call them 'synthetic neoplasms'; and as the wording suggests, this does not just imply that they are man-made, but also that they are, in material terms, composites. In fact, Cronenberg's pods are described in the movie as being hybrid creatures that crossbreed parts of different organisms, clearly pointing to what Kevin Kelly has defined as 'neo-biological'.[10]

Hieronymus Bosch's extraordinary depictions of hybrid creatures in the 16th century can be seen as an important precedent for such neoplasms. In a similar way, Pieter Bruegel, who borrowed and adapted a number of Bosch's visions, produced paintings richly inhabited with bizarre half-man, half-animal, half-vegetable beings. Later, in the 17th century, the *Amorphous Monster*[11] drawn by Fortunius Licetus became a formal predecessor of work that was to be carried out in the 20th century which, even though not always implying life, could be considered neoplasmatic. Artists such as Louise Bourgeois put forward a series of hybrid plasms[12] that expressed a strong carnal eroticism of living flesh.

In fact, one of the most critical features of all synthetic neoplasms is flesh. To explore this, one has to understand flesh as an extended meaning of skin and, accordingly, skin not as a surface or membrane, but rather like 'a place of minglings',[13] as the English theorist Steve Connor has put it. This implies a sense of three-dimensionality that is manifest through the nakedness and materiality of skin in which embedded matter, along with a variety of wrinkles, bulges and orifices mark their presence, in turn influencing the flesh's texture and colour.

In the case of Cronenberg's game-pods there is an undefined lightness and sense of transparency noticeable on the skin. The fact that the game-pods are assembled from genetically engineered amphibian organs and limbs, requiring an outer skin that ties them together, might help in explaining this feature. Their synthetic nature suggests that the skin is very likely to be artificially grown; and since pigmented skin is still difficult to produce in vitro – one is here deliberately comparing scientific evidence with fictional imagery – one could imagine that the game-pods most probably lack colour altogether. In other words, the absence of pigmentation stigmatises them with being albino, a phenomenon that detaches them from a long-standing racial argument of skin colour that has been so significant in our cultural history.

Another relevant physiological feature of the game-pods has to do with their unclear gender. In the movie they are presented with

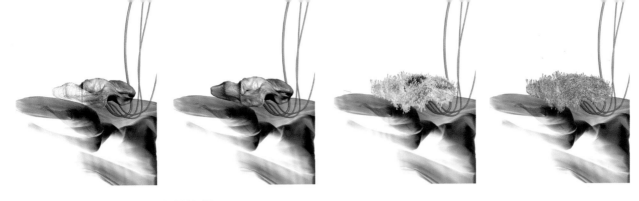

Stefanie Surjo, Synthetic pet growth, 2004–05
Drawings showing the evolution of hair growth on an artificial pet.

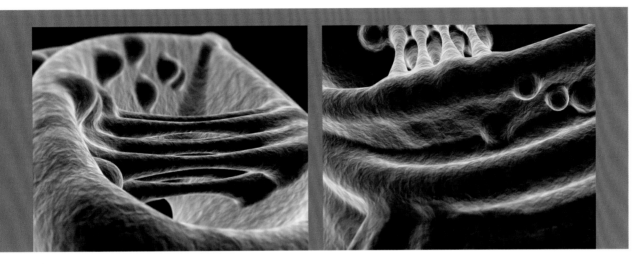

Samuel White, Cellular Structure, 2003–04
Rendered view at the microscopic scale of artificially grown human skin cells – keratynocites. Different formations emerge from the surface as nodes of cell culture and distribution of nutrients and antibodies. At a macro scale the differentiated distribution of cells is imperceptible. Moving in from macro to micro, the apparent ordered structure of the cell laboratory dissolves into roughly structured hierarchies and forms. At the nano scale, supreme control of the cell environment is acquired while the heterogeneous quirks of form are maintained.

ambivalent sexual connotations[14] that cannot be explained through the traditional feminist discourse on gender difference. If the recesses and nipple-like protrusions, as well as the colour and lack of muscular structure, seem somehow female, the impenetrability and resistance is more likely to be male.[15] Hence the game-pods give the impression of being multi-gendered, or perhaps something else that fits with Donna Haraway's argument of a post-gendered world.[16]

Furthermore, it is worth mentioning the game-pods' highly sensitive skin in which sensations seem topologically and dermatologically determined. This is in a passive and involuntary way, as the pods just react to external pressures when players trigger the game to start. Without being touched they seem incapable of acting by themselves. In her book *Skin*, the German cultural historian Claudia Benthien pointed out a basic difference between the notion of feeling and touch,[17] which indicates in this case the inherent separation between the player's exploratory activity of touch and the pod's inactivity of skin feelings. In the film this is repeatedly seen in the way Allegra Geller handles the game-pods. Her recurrent strokes imply much more than a simple demonstration of care or functional turning on and off; she is actually massaging, or better, kneading them. Symbolically, this represents an inclusive act that does not separate the pulp from body or skin; on the contrary, it

Frank Tjepkema, Artificial plant for Droog, 1996
Plastic and rubber; 50 x 50 x 15 cm.

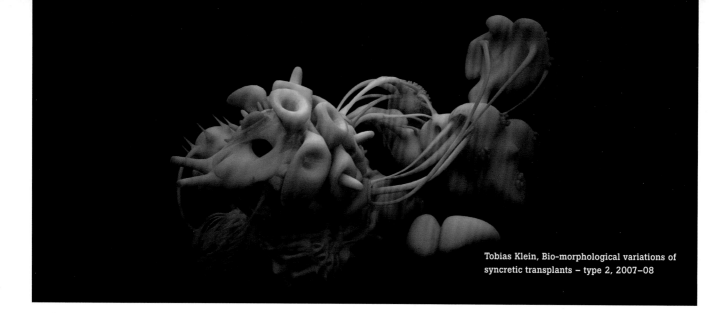

Tobias Klein, Bio-morphological variations of syncretic transplants – type 2, 2007–08

merges the inner and outer side of neoplasms into a continuous intermingling of substance. Having in mind the earlier definition of synthetic neoplasms, it is right to say that the game-pods are synthetic in a double sense: through the man-made composition of different organic flesh, and the symbolic act of kneading where distinct matter is merged into a synthetic whole. Connor's descriptions in *The Book of Skin* suggest that kneading also entails an energising process in which the vitality of the user's body is passed on to what is being kneaded, turning it into a kind of 'living flesh'.[18] 'It is not the final shape of the model, but the shapeliness, the torque or tension of contour in it, the power of being given and retaining shape of the material of which it has been formed, that contains its inner virtue. The skin is the medium and the aim for the formation of this imagery flesh, this worked and working transubstance.'[19]

The idea of a working 'transubstance' reinforces the notion of depth in the synthetic neoplasms' three-dimensional flesh. Earlier, the transparent quality of the game-pods' skin was highlighted when describing them as albino. But one wonders what kind of transparency this really is when, for instance, the underlying vascular system marks its presence on the skin in an indistinguishable manner. Flesh is in this case neither opaque nor transparent. Yet the physical condition of having *in*-corporated matter in the dermis that is visible through the trans-*lucent* epidermis makes such neoplasms become what one could define as 'inlucent' – a condition of embedded matter that goes beyond the Modernist dualism of opacity–transparency and the more contemporary notion of translucency. One could then argue that kneading the game-pods is a way to enhance the tactile perception of an *inlucent transubstance* of flesh.

Cronenberg's neoplasms, however, denote another feature that distinguishes them mostly from any of their relatives: their networked condition, which is so vital for

them to come alive. His pods are parasitic creatures that use the energy of human beings as their power supply, at the same time being biological prosthetics that extend the human body to the virtual realm. Oron Catts and Ionat Zurr at SymbioticA have defined this as a state of 'partial life'.[20] Unlike other neoplasms, Cronenberg's game-pods are ultimately connected, temporarily inhabiting the body of the player, as well as being inhabited by it. Two biological systems are intermingled here, crossbreeding organic and artificial life. They recall HR Giger's Biomechanoids series, which shows organisms that are multi-linked, in this case to a non-biological apparatus. Perhaps what underlines this trend of physically connecting the human body to machines, artificial organisms, or even other human bodies, and extending the mind into a virtual world while giving up the capacity to control the real body left behind, is the reflection of a wider and more profound condition that Jean Baudrillard called the '"proteinic" era of networks', a circumstance in which 'connections, contact, contiguity, feedback and generalized interface … [go] with the universe of communication'.[21]

Although Cronenberg's game-pods are only networked with each other, their interfacial existence is dependent on precisely these factors; they imply a biotechnological hyper-connectivity bounded by flesh. The intra-networking of his synthetic neoplasms with the players blurs the traditional boundaries of corporeality in which the human body's flesh becomes an extension of the neoplasm's flesh and vice versa. This means that the players' bodies do not just engage in a new sensory interplay with the flesh of other bodies, but also acquire a new sense of being and place. In a speculative manner, one could then assume that the players of *eXistenZ* experience the foreign body of the neoplasm with a new type of existential proximity that prompts an unavoidable strain between the feeling of *having flesh* (implying the physical body), *being flesh* (implying a sense of embodiment), and *becoming flesh* (implying the embodiment of the foreign body of the game-pod).[22]

In conclusion, it is worth restating the significance of Cronenberg's almost 10-year-old movie *eXistenZ* as a still contemporary paradigm that exposes deep-rooted fears and fascinations in popular culture about the complete biologicalisation of our world. But by putting forward the game-pods, Cronenberg not just anticipated a new hybridism between biological and non-biological systems, but also a

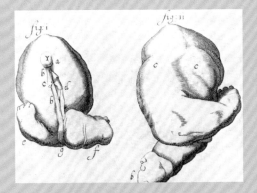

Fortunius Licetus, *Amorphous Monster*, 1665
Licetus published *De Monstruorum Natura* in 1616, in which he extensively studied malformations of the embryo. By describing and analysing various monsters both in a real and imaginary way, he searched for the causes of such manifestations. His scientific approach differed from others at the time, as he did not consider monsters as a divine punishment, but rather as a fantastical rarity.

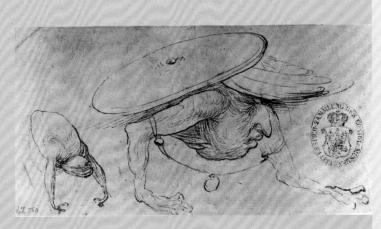

Hieronymus Bosch, *Human head pacing rightwards on animal legs – on the left a creature resembling a paddock on two long legs*, c 1450–1516
Kupferstichkabinett, Staatliche Museen zu Berlin. Brown ink on red coloured paper; 8.6 x 18.2 cm.

Pieter Bruegel the Elder, *Dulle Griet (Mad Meg) – Detail of various monsters*, 1564
Museum Mayer van den Berg, Antwerp, Belgium. Oil on canvas; 117 x 162 cm.

Louise Bourgeois, *Lair*, 1963
Latex; 24.1 x 42.5 x 36.5 cm.

Louise Bourgeois, *Le Regard*, 1966
Latex and cloth; 12.7 x 39.3 x 36.8 cm.

Louise Bourgeois, *Double Negative*, 1963
Latex over plaster; 49.2 x 95.2 x 79.6 cm.

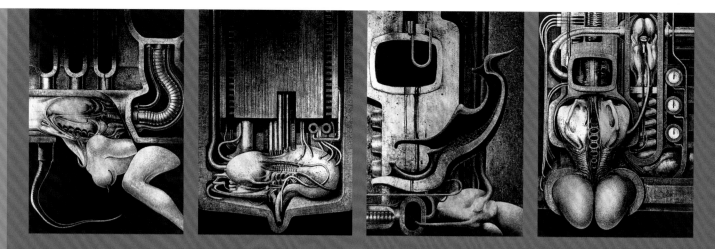

HR Giger, *Biomechanoid nos 99, 101, 103, 104*, 1969
Silkscreen, black on silver; 110 x 80 cm. Editions of 100 from the portfolio, Biomechanoiden.

new experiential dimension and haptic relationship between the human body and its surrounding, which stands in opposition to the previous hegemony of vision that determined so much of the 20th-century built environment. The game-pods reflect, most of all, what is defined as synthetic neoplasms, instigating a completely new aesthetic argument in design in which grotesque, ugly and even disgusting conditions can be accepted as valid criteria. They also challenge traditional notions of programme and technology, and raise fundamental questions of how, who and where such things can be created. Ultimately they launch a very important debate on how we will face the prospect of a semi-living architecture. ∆

Notes

1. This is an expression originally used by Oron Catts and Ionat Zurr of the Tissue Culture and Art Project (TC&A). See www.tca.uwa.edu.au/extra/extra-ear.html.
2. Director: David Cronenberg; Production: Screenventures XXIV Production Ltd/Alliance Atlantis Company and Existence Productions Limited, 1999.
3. This is a definition that Lynn uses to describe the pre-objectual state of blobs. See Greg Lynn, 'Blob tectonics, or why tectonics is square and topology is groovy', in *Folds, Bodies and Blobs: Collected Essays*, La Lettre Volée (Brussels), 1998, pp 170–1.
4. This is evident in the film when the game-pods are featured being ill and infected.
5. For more on Bataille's '*informe*', see Yve-Alain Bois and Rosalind Krauss, *Formless: A User's Guide*, Zone Books (New York), 1997.
6. This is an expression originally used by Oron Catts and Ionat Zurr of the Tissue Culture and Art Project (TC&A). See www.tca.uwa.edu.au/extra/extra-ear.html.
7. According to the *Oxford English Dictionary* the suffix 'plasm' forms 'nouns denoting shapeless or mouldable substances, esp. (in biology) kinds of protoplasm or intracellular ground substance'.
8. *Encyclopaedia Britannica*, Deluxe Edition, CD, 2004.
9. The suffix 'plasmatic' is deliberately used instead of 'plasmic'. According to the *Oxford English Dictionary* plasmatic denotes 'the power

of giving shape or form', as well as 'relating to the formation of tissue', while plasmic refers specifically to 'the nature of plasm or plasma' in strictly biological terms.
10. See Kelly's predictions of a post-biological civilisation in which almost everything will be infused with principles of bio-logic. Kevin Kelly, *Out of Control: The New Biology of Machines*, Fourth Estate (London), 1994, p 606.
11. For more on this see Ian McCormick's 'Encyclopedia of the Marvelous, the Monstrous, and the Grotesque' at http://easyweb.easynet.co.uk/~ian.mccormick/encyclop.htm.
12. According to the *Oxford English Dictionary* the noun 'plasm' refers to 'a mould or matrix in which something is cast or formed'.
13. Steve Connor, *The Book of Skin*, Reaktion Books (London), 2004, p 26.
14. Apart from the eroticism of touching the game-pods, which is evident when Allegra has to stimulate them in order to 'turn them on', the procedure of introducing their umbilical cord into the player's bioports (an orifice on his spine) is relevant. There is a sense of penetration that particularly in Ted Pikul's case can be seen as an inherently masculine attribute that feminises his male body.
15. I am here interpreting Claudia Benthien's analysis about male and female skin. See the chapter 'Armoured Skin and Birthmarks' in Claudia Benthien, *Skin: On the Cultural Border Between Self and the World*, Columbia University Press (New York), 2002, pp 133–43.
16. Donna Haraway, *Simians, Cyborgs, and Women: The Reinvention of Nature*, Free Association Books Ltd (London), 1991, p 150.
17. Benthien op cit, pp 198–200.
18. Connor op cit, p 226.
19. Ibid.
20. This again is an expression originally used by Oron Catts and Ionat Zurr. See www.tca.uwa.edu.au/extra/extra-ear.html.
21. Jean Baudrillard, 'The ecstasy of communication', in Hal Foster (ed), *The Anti-Aesthetic: Essays on Postmodern Culture*, Bay Press (Seattle, WA), 1983, p 127.
22. This thought is based on ML Lyon's and JM Barbalet's argument on the implicit duality between 'having and being a body'. For more see ML Lyon and JM Barbalch, 'Society's body: emotion and "somatization" of social theory', in Thomas J Csordas (ed), *Embodiment and Experience: The Existential Ground of Culture and Self*, Cambridge University Press (Cambridge), 2003, p 56.

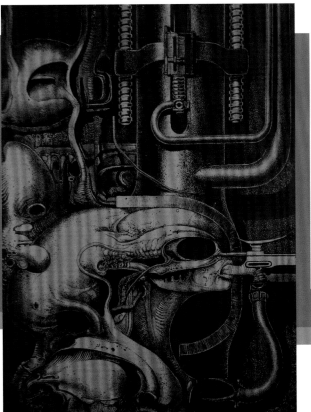

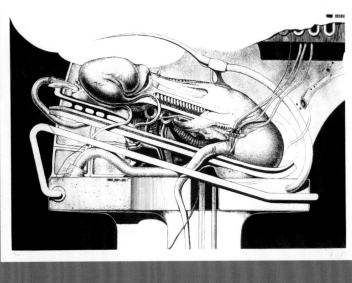

HR Giger, *Plan for Biomechanoid I – no. 107,* **1969**
Silkscreen, black on silver; 110 x 80 cm. Edition of 100
from the Biomechanoiden portfolio.

HR Giger, *Biomechanoid no. 95,* **1969**
Silkscreen, black on silver; 110 x 80 cm. Edition
of 100 from the Biomechanoiden portfolio.

HR Giger, *Plan for Biomechanoid II – no. 108,* **1969**
Silkscreen, black on silver; 110 x 80 cm. Edition of 100
from the Biomechanoiden portfolio.

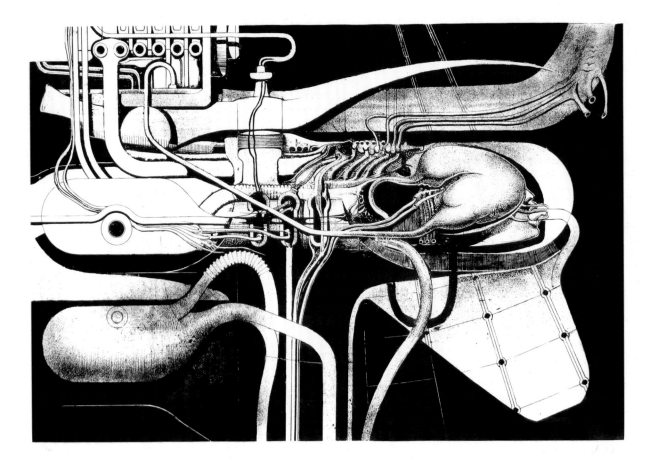

Density Fields in Viscous Bodies

Taking raw data of a human MRI (magnetic resonance imaging) scan as a starting point, **Tobias Klein** reimagines the body in a new viscous stage where the body's inner and outer layers are irrelevant and it becomes a fluctuating variable in concentrated mass and matter.

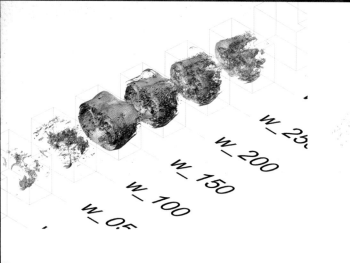

Tobias Klein, Density Fields in Viscous Bodies, 2007–08

top: Virtual organs are redesigned as syncretic transplants, exploring a visceral state of fluctuation between real and virtual flesh components.
centre: Syncretic transplants are hybrid natural–artificial mutations within newly created viscous bodies.
bottom: The body is dissected, projected and analysed in a gradient of density fields generated from the MRI scans.

The Density Fields in Viscous Bodies research project explores the human body as a new ecology of densities.[1] The dissolution of the body's anatomical boundaries allows the reconsideration and recreation of it as a new physical territory in constant flux and change. It questions the common representations of the body in the digital realm as a series of surfaces and layers, and creates a potentially new status where the modulation of the body's inner and outer surfaces becomes irrelevant. By using advanced medical visualisation techniques as both method and tool to redesign the body with variable intensities of matter, the obsolete notion of a finite body is exposed in favour of a new type of body-space that is, above all, a viscous field of variable concentrations of mass and matter.

The project is sited within the seamless transitional fluctuation of a real/virtual body, an extended and projected body, where the traditional dichotomy between inner and outer space is dissolved. Derived from the use of non-invasive visualisation techniques, it attempts to reverse-engineer the understanding of the body within the emergent immersive environment of a virtual continuum. Raw data of a human MRI (magnetic resonance imaging) scan is taken as a starting point.[2] Here, digital processes are used to create three-dimensional images from the inside of the body, as a result of interactive static and variable gradients of magnetic fields. In addition, data is generated and assembled with the use of the 2DFT (Two-Dimensional Fourier Transform) technique that incorporates slice selection, in which a magnetic gradient is applied during the radio frequency pulse.

The resulting images are composed of a number of spatial frequencies at differing orientations where 'space' is generated through interlocking density fields. The slices of the MRI scan are then used to reinvest a newly created structure of virtual organs, a sort of syncretic transplant that permits the emergence of a visceral state of fluctuation between real and virtual flesh components. This transformation, from a Euclidean described solid body to a field of informed particles, described in medical terms as voxels,[3] delineates new typologies of viscous bodies that are constantly readdressed, adjusted and, ultimately, modified.[4] ⚙

Notes

1. The project, originally entitled Soft Immortality, was developed in the context of the MArch bolt-on at the Bartlett School of Architecture, UCL, with the support of Neil Spiller and Phil Watson, in 2007–08. It follows a broader investigation into the virtual condensation of actual and augmented spaces that started with the diploma thesis 'Synthetic Syncretism' developed two years earlier in Unit 20 under the supervision of Marjan Colletti and Shaun Murray.

2. According to the Oxford Concise Medical Dictionary, MRI is 'a diagnostic technique based on analysis of the absorption and transmission of high-frequency radio waves by the water molecules in tissues placed in a strong magnetic field. Using modern high-speed computers, this analysis can be used to "map out" the variation in tissue signals in any place and thus produce images of the tissues. It is particularly useful for examining the central nervous system and musculoskeletal system, and to a lesser extent the chest and abdomen. MRI can be used for the non-invasive diagnosis and treatment planning of a wide range of diseases, including cancer: it has the advantage that it does not use potentially harmful ionizing radiation, such as X-rays.' Elizabeth A Martin (ed), Concise Medical Dictionary (1980), 5th edn, Oxford University Press (Oxford), 1998, p 387.

3. A voxel is 'the volume of tissue in a body that is represented by a pixel in a cross-sectional image'. Ibid, p 705.

4. Voxels can contain multiple scalar values that are essentially vector data. In the case of ultrasound scans with B-mode and Doppler data, density and volumetric flow rate are captured as separate channels of data relating to the same voxel positions. This allows an informed mouldable and flexible model of space, and enables objects to become spatial fragments that are no longer described in a static fashion, but are more fields in constant shift within a virtual continuum.

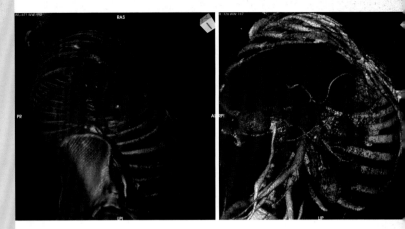

Cross-sectional perspectives of the author's body generated from MRI scans.

Physical model (Rapid Prototype, Objet) of a syncretic transplant. A prosthetic gradient is created in which the observer is shifting around variable density fields of environmentally looped vectors determined by light and kinetic impulses.

The choreography of light through the kinetic installation creates permutations determined by density, translucency and reflection. The body's densities are imaged, digitised, manipulated, projected and reimagined, creating a tentative four-dimensional representation: a simulacrum.

Designer

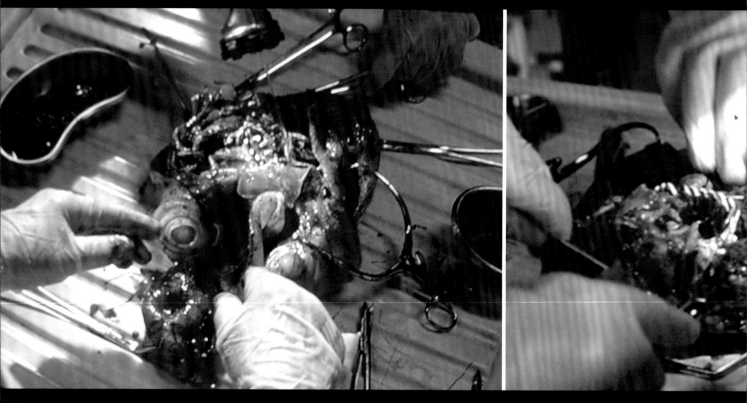

The advances of ever more complex visualisation and 3-D modelling techniques in medicine have brought a new emphasis to surgery in which the surgeon's role has become more concerned with design than reconstruction, as the aesthetic of the finished human product becomes the main focus and reason for surgery. **Marcos Cruz** looks at some art projects that have questioned and extended this application of surgery and design, as well as asking what the implications are for architecture.

There has been much discussion about the increasing interdisciplinary synthesis between various research disciplines, but less said about the emergence of new professions that result from contemporary advances in biomedical sciences, especially in respect of the impact of design in these fields. In this context, the creation of synthetic neoplasms[1] as shown in David Cronenberg's movie *eXistenZ* (1999)[2] is a noteworthy example, prompting fundamental questions about where and how the featured game-pods are created, and who the designer behind such hybrid constructs is: a professional, who uses tools and techniques, as well as possessing expertise that certainly goes beyond the training of a conventional surgeon, extending to the design of 'semi-living' conditions.[3]

Surgeons

David Cronenberg, *eXistenZ*, 1999
Game–pod surgery performed in a ski club.

The Surgeon as a Sculptor

To contemplate the evolution of this new professional figure it is worth reflecting on the practice of the great German-Jewish plastic surgeon Jacques Joseph and his invention of the Senn-Joseph flap technique[4] that enabled him to reconstruct the face of a patient who had lost half of his during the Crimean War. Without surgical precedent and using very rudimentary instruments, Joseph anticipated the results of the procedure using a virtual template that he conjured up through the power of his imagination alone, and his pioneering method is still used today in the practice of reconstructive surgery. Although the technique was born of honourable intentions, Joseph's intervention raised questions about the aesthetic parameters he was following during the reconstruction procedure, which exposed latent cultural anxieties about the surgeon's instrumental power to redesign the human body, such as those conjectures made by the medical historian Sander Gilman who questioned the validity of a surgeon as a sculptor.[5]

The American novelist Mary Higgins Clark explained this functional dualism, of artist and surgical technician, as the 'Pygmalion fantasy' of a surgeon,[6] referring to the figure of a sculptor in Greek mythology who falls in love with his own creation and wishes to bring it to life. The highly subjective nature implicit in such an act suggests the plastic surgeon as possessing 'dangerous' powers of inflicting deliberately chosen parameters that enable him to work outside the confines of medical ethos and, in turn, challenges the conduct of certain surgical interventions within the medical sciences. This is of particular importance when considering how the impact of rapidly emerging technological advances is enabling contemporary surgeons to perform ever more complex and, until now, unimaginable operations. Ultimately, these procedures could lead to fully redesigning the human body, or even to the creation of completely new living beings, as shown in Patricia Piccinini's provocative artwork *Science Story* (2001).

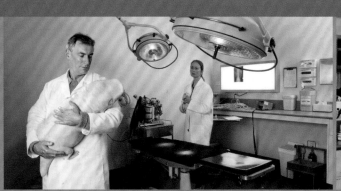

Patricia Piccinini, *Science Story Part 1: Laboratory Procedures*, 2001
C-Type photograph; 100 x 200 cm.

Patricia Piccinini, *Science Story Part 2: Ethical Issues*, 2001
C-Type photograph; 100 x 200 cm.

Patricia Piccinini, *Science Story Part 3: Research Methods*, 2001
C-Type photograph; 100 x 200cm.

Patricia Piccinini, *Science Story Part 4: Thesis and Conclusions*, 2001
C-Type photograph; 100 x 200 cm.

The speed of technological progress is reflected in the increasing sub-specialisation within the practice of plastic surgery, which has led to the loss of an overview regarding what is happening within the field as a whole. The exclusive territories of plastic, aesthetic, cosmetic and reconstructive surgeons are being challenged by developments in other surgical, medical and allied-medical specialities such as transplant, dermatological and cosmetic surgery, along with the specific practice of cosmetic dermatologists, aestheticians or cosmeticians currently exploring the emerging territory of anatomical design.[7] This blurring of professional boundaries provokes further discussion about deontological priorities, which distinguishes between an understanding of medicine that 'does not acknowledge "beauty" as one of its goals ... [or] in which the creation of a "beautiful" face and body is asserted as a legitimate medical goal'.[8] In other words, it is a debate that goes beyond the implication of the surgeon's practice as a reconstructive sculptor, introducing design as a new method and conduct.

The Operating Theatre as an Art Studio or Workshop

The French multimedia artist Orlan employed surgeons to transform her aesthetic identity into one of her own creation during a series of operation performances in which she considered her flesh to be the artist's canvas, and effectively surrendered her body as an object of design. The sci-fi clinician Rachel Armstrong described it as 'the beginning of a new phenomenon in medicine: designer anatomy',[9] a concept that precedes the idea of Designer Surgeons. Orlan's challenge to the medical profession, however, went beyond the confines of medical aesthetics. She set a new politics for the operating theatre where surgery became a mediatic event and the operating theatre was subverted to become a new kind of art studio, democratising the place of surgical practice. It is already a quite common practice that physicians, whether acknowledged specialists or not, can carry out surgery, especially plastic surgery, away from the visible control of medical institutions.[10] This means that surgery is returning to its once controversial professional state, in which almost any practitioner could undertake operations at any site or place.

This decentring of surgical control is revealed in Cronenberg's *eXistenZ* with a variety of backyard environments in which surgery takes place, where unconventional sites are used to treat and operate the game-pods, including a car mechanic's workshop, a ski club and a converted barn.[11] These places do not just host a series of rather suspect individuals who give the impression of having the expertise of surgeons, but also challenge the clandestine and grotesque nature of Cronenberg's neoplasms with a technological sophistication required in such design and manufacturing processes, most of which is already available today.

Design of Synthetic Neoplasms:
New Methods of Planning in Surgery

Scale is a fundamental precondition of designing synthetic neoplasms. Recent developments in biological and medical sciences have shown that molecular design has the potential to manipulate genetic codes that can alter cellular growth as well as the functions of cells. When combined with nanotechnological devices, it is possible, for example, to revitalise or manipulate the longevity of living systems. Research on biomaterials has shown how the growth of natural or artificial organs and skin tissue can be accomplished on a cellular level by combining biological systems and synthetic materials.[12] Contemporary surgery has also reached the point where the transplant of organs and tissue has become a daily practice. Immunological as well as technical problems, such as keeping organs alive, and the assembling of the different connective organs or ducts within the host body, have gradually been overcome – see performance artist Stelarc's recent implant of his Extra Ear.[13]

Micro-machinery and larger-scale devices are also being inserted in the body, hybridising human flesh with machine supplements – see Kevin Warwick's recent implant.[14] The manufacturing of biocompatible prosthetics, advances in visualisation techniques, and high-precision operation tools such as the da Vinci Surgical System[15] are increasingly been implemented in surgery with the help of complex computer software. Furthermore, the possibility of planning and rehearsing the operations through new 2-D/3-D digital techniques is allowing surgery for completely unprecedented operations; a realisation that the American historian Timothy Lenoir recognised is giving medicine not just immense predictive, but also experimental, power,[16] which is obviously of great importance for the creation of new and synthetic life.[17]

The Surgeon as a Technician Versus the Surgeon as a Designer

Designer surgery, however, is currently beyond the scope of traditional medical education and practice.[18] As Lenoir has shown, apart from more conventional 'background knowledge in the texts and practices of anatomy, biochemistry, physiology, and pathology, including some traditional practices from earlier generations … new fields such as biophysics, computer graphics and animation, biorobotics, and mechanical and biomedical engineering' are necessary. 'They will also need to be aware of the importance of network services and bandwidth issues as enabling components of their practice.'[19] That means that such evolution is forcing 'the last generation's heroic surgeon' like Joseph to be upgraded to a new type of 'techno-supersurgeon' as Lenoir has suggested,[20] simultaneously imposing an inevitable division of the profession into a multitude of different yet complementary professional experts.

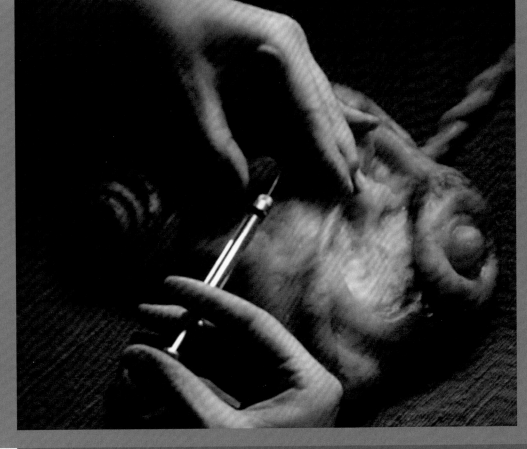

David Cronenberg, *eXistenZ*, 1999
An infected game-pod being injected with anti-sporal disinfectant. Will this also be necessary in a future semi-living architecture?

The creation of a supersurgeon has further implications in as much as '… creativity will be of a different sort, as many of the functions now internalised by surgeons are externalised into packaged surgical design tools just as computer-aided design packages such as AutoCAD, 3D Studio Max, or Maya have reconfigured the training, design practices and creativity of architects. Some surgeons with access to resources will undoubtedly engage in high-level surgical design work, but that process will be mediated in teamwork involving software engineers, robotics experts, and a host of others.'[21]

What is significant in this comment is that Lenoir predicts a multi-task performance in the surgeon's practice that involves hands-on operations and simultaneously the act of design. That these are performed by more than one single surgeon suggests a split in the profession, that brings about mutually dependent surgeons who work with a team of other specialists, including traditional surgeons, and new types of designer surgeons. The former stand in the tradition of surgeons as interventionist agents who are able to restore and alter the human body, whereas the latter envision and prepare the operations in terms of modelling and visualisation techniques. Although familiar with practical operation procedures and in direct contact with interventionist surgeons at all times, such surgeons remain rather theoretical and conceptual, and have the crucial responsibility to overview the whole process. This is clearly seen in *eXistenZ* in the role of Allegra Geller, who is the 'designer' of the game-pods without, however, being able to manufacture and operate them. In other words, to create Cronenberg's synthetic neoplasms the traditional interventionist surgeon as a remodeller and reconstructor complements the job of the designer surgeon as planner and modeller.[22]

In the end it is worth questioning what the importance of all this is for architecture and how this might affect the way in which we understand our profession in a near future where our built environment might become hybridised with biological systems that require medical interventions. Considering the complexity and scientific expertise that will be inherent to such systems, which a designer is by default not trained to handle, one has to assume that the role of surgeons who increasingly embrace new tools of design will become of particular relevance. On the other hand, architects and designers are utilising news tools, such as sophisticated CAD/CAM processes that were originally implemented in the medical sciences,[23] as well as considering completely new scales of operation that they acknowledge are becoming of ever growing importance for their projects. In fact, their workstations are becoming conspicuously similar to those used in contemporary surgery.

William Mitchell gives an interesting account of the potential intermingling of different work procedures and scales in a variety of research fields, arguing that:

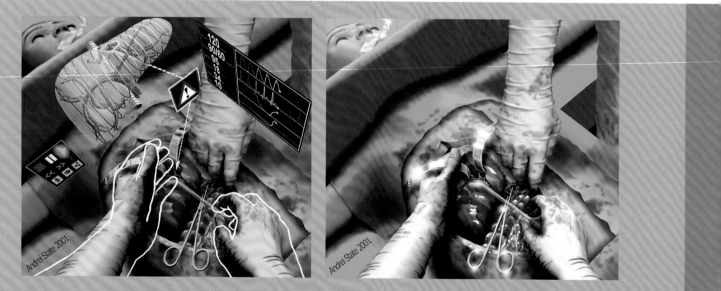

Henry Fuchs, Greg Welch and Andries Van Dam, Immersive electronic books for teaching surgical procedures, University of North Carolina and Brown University, 2002–04
The aim of this joint research project is the development of a new paradigm for teaching surgical procedures through immersive electronic books that allow surgeons to witness and explore (in time and space) a past surgical procedure as if they were there, with the added benefit of integrated instructions from the original surgeon or another instructor, as well as incorporated 3-D illustrations, annotations and relevant medical metadata. The trainees are able to freely and naturally walk around a life-sized, high-fidelity, 3-D graphical reconstruction of the original time-varying events. Left: Surgeon's view during emergency surgery involving a blunt liver trauma. Right: Trainee's view within an immersive time machine with VCR-like controls and medical annotations. The trainee's hands are captured in real time and merged into the reconstructed event as white outlines (artist's impressions). Images created by Andrei State, Senior Research Scientist at the Department of Computer Science, University of North Carolina, 2001.

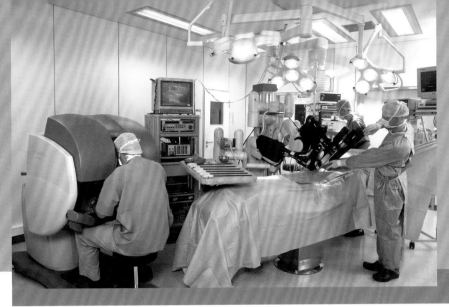

Intuitive Surgical, Inc, da Vinci Surgical System, Dresden, Germany, 2000
Using the da Vinci Surgical System, the surgeon operates at a distance of 3 to 4.5 metres (10 to 15 feet) from the patient, while ergonomically seated at a console viewing a 3-D image of the surgical field. The surgeon's fingers grasp the master controls below the display, with hands and wrists naturally positioned relative to his or her eyes. In a master–slave relationship, the system seamlessly translates the surgeon's hand, wrist and finger movements into precise, real-time movements of surgical instruments inside the patient.

Today, [traditional] scale chauvinism makes little sense. The solution to a given design problem might be found at any scale or combination of scales … It makes even less sense to draw sharp distinctions between non-living and living systems. As biology, materials science, mechanical engineering, and electronics all get down to the molecular scale, they deal with the same types and sizes of structures, and there is a growing crossover of interests and goals. As biologists engage ideas of modular recombination, slicing, and cloning, they begin to think like designers. Conversely, as designers tentatively embrace concepts of emergence, self-organization, self-assembly, and self-replication, they start to sound like biologists. Increasingly, the CAD console meets the wet lab, and the circuit shop keeps company with the chemistry bench.[24]

With this comment, Mitchell does not just call to mind a professional fusion that is already in place with the work of biochemists and bioengineers, for example, but also clearly predicts the advent of Designer Surgeons who have already conquered sufficient freedom in terms of ethics, work place and know-how (combining simultaneously scientific and artistic work methodologies) in order to realise the biologicalisation of architecture that so many envision. Δ

Notes
1. The concept of synthetic neoplasms is discussed in another article in this issue: see 'Synthetic Neoplasms', pp 36–43.
2. Director: David Cronenberg; Production: Screenventures XXIV Production Ltd/Alliance Atlantis Company and Existence Productions Limited, 1999.
3. This expression was originally used by Oron Catts and Ionat Zurr of the Tissue Culture and Art Project (TC&A). See www.tca.uwa.edu.au/extra/extra-ear.html.
4. A primitive version of this technique was invented by Nicholas Senn in 1903 and later accomplished by Jacques Joseph in 1918 without having any knowledge of his predecessor. See Paul Natvig, *Jacques Joseph: Surgical Sculptor*, WB Saunders Company (Philadelphia, PA), 1982, p 10.

5. Gilman talks about this problem when referring to the relationship between the surgeon as a sculptor and the patient as a classical statue. See Sander L Gilman, *Making the Body Beautiful: A Cultural History of Aesthetic Surgery*, Princeton University Press (Princeton, NJ), 1999, p 235.
6. Ibid, p 318.
7. Gilman lists numerous specialisations, including mentoplasty, otoplasty, blepharoplasty, rhytidectomy, rhinoplasty, brachioplasty, mammaplasty, matopexy, posthioplasty, lipectomy, gynecomastia, abdominoplasty and more general terms such as ophthalmic surgery and otorhinolaryngologic surgery. Ibid, pp 5–7.
8. See the passage 'Why is it Aesthetic Surgery?' in Chapter 1, ibid, pp 8–16.
9. Rachel Armstrong, 'Anger, art and medicine: Working with Orlan', in Joanna Zylinska (ed), *The Cyborg Experiments: The Extensions of the Body in the Media Age*, Continuum (London), 2002, p 173.
10. See Gilman op cit, p 6.
11. In *eXistenZ* the backyard workshop of a petrol station is used to implant bioports in the human spine, necessary to plug the game-pods into the player's body. A ski club, on the other hand, is the environment where game-pods can be surgically repaired, while a barn is transformed into a factory where mutated amphibians are dissected, their organs extirpated, redistributed and then reassembled into newly created synthetic organisms.
12. See Buddy D Ratner, Allan S Hoffman, Frederick J Schoen and Jack E Lemons, *Biomaterials Science: An Introduction to Materials in Medicine*, Academic Press Inc, 1996, p 1.
13. See http://www.sial.rmit.edu.au/Projects/Stelarc_Tissue_Culture_and_Art.php.
14. For more about Warwick's implants, see http://www.kevinwarwick.com/.
15. While at SRI (formerly the Stanford Research Institute), Philip Green was instrumental in the initial development of this medical device for use on the battlefields. This eventually led to the design of the surgical robot used in operating rooms all over the world, which is now known as the da Vinci Surgical System and produced by Intuitive Surgical, Inc.
16. See Timothy Lenoir, 'The virtual Surgeon: Operating on the data in an age of medialization', in Phillip Thurtle and Robert E Mitchell (eds), *Semiotic Flesh: Information and the Human Body*, University of Washington Press, 2002, p. 28.
17. Ibid.
18. Ibid, pp 43–4.
19. Ibid.
20. Ibid, p 43.
21. Ibid, p 44.
22. The removal of the prefix 're' in common terms such as re-construct or re-build represents a meaningful change in attitude and performance of the traditional surgical practice and changes it into a new role of Designer Surgeon.
23. It is not a coincidence that the first CAD/CAM machines used at the Bartlett School of Architecture where purchased second-hand from the medical department at UCL where they were originally used to produce complex bone prosthetics.
24. William J Mitchell, *ME++: The Cyborg Self and the Networked City*, MIT Press (Cambridge, MA), 2003, pp 71–2.

Human Cloning

Human cloning is positioned at the edge of the real and the imaginary, proving the extreme scenario for the possible and the acceptable. Here, **Nicola Haines'** proposal for a human cloning clinic situated in the Arsenale in Venice goes beyond traditional modes of representation, suggesting new codes and thus a new drawing language that combines scientific with architectural data.

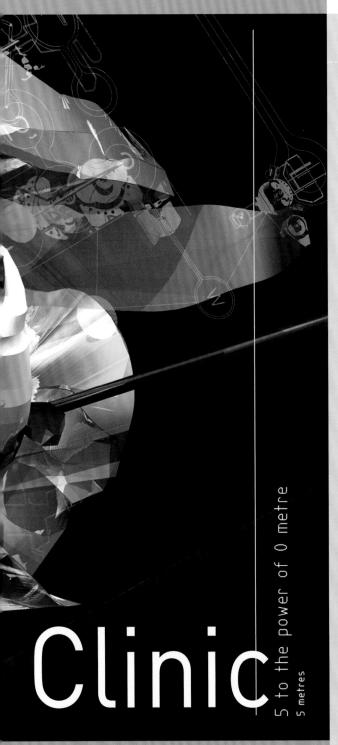

Located in the Arsenale in Venice, this project for a human cloning clinic[1] benefits from this ex-naval structure's inherent qualities of secrecy, restriction and military screening. The design is based on the seven basic steps essential to the successful cloning of a person:

1. Human cell growth media: cells of one tissue type are harvested from the donor.
2. Minimal media: cells are controlled to a quiescent state, and allowed to live but not to divide.
3. Separation area: the nucleus is removed from another source of human eggs.
4. Fusion: cells from the quiescent state are fused with the 'empty' egg cell.
5. The fused eggs are shocked with electricity to 're-boot' the human genetic programme, tricking the egg into believing it has been fertilised by sperm.
6. Cell growth media: the embryos are allowed to grow and divide.
7. Implantation area: the embryos are implanted into human mothers, carried to term and born naturally.

Each of these seven stages has been formalised as a single laboratory that performs a specific function in the overall system. The location and spatial relationship between each of the laboratories reflects their stage within the cloning machine. They are combined with the paths of specialist technicians, cleaners and maintenance personnel, along with the potential offspring's parents in a way that blurs the usually private moment of conception with public event. In parallel, a notation specific to genetics is incorporated into an architectural language to act as a diagrammatic tool for allocating space.

The proposed clinic is examined at a variety of radically differing scales. Cloning operates on a microscopic level, therefore the 'micro-world' is considered in as much detail as the urban. It is an experimental proposal that aims to fuse scientific language with architectural process – the normally natural event of conception with the artificial – and to address the delicate balance between organic cycles and commoditisation.

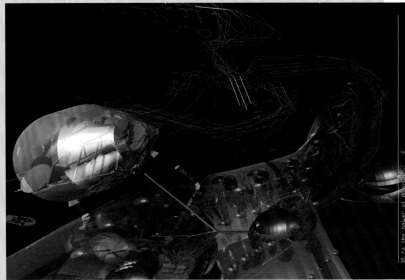

Clinic

5 to the power of 0 metre

5 metres

Nicola Haines, Human Cloning Clinic, Arsenale, Venice, 1998–99
A 'mother' embryo sorter dispersing cells to micro sacks. Scale: 5 to the power of 0 metres.

A feeder component adjusting hydration levels within the micro embryo sacks.
Scale 10 to the power of –2.

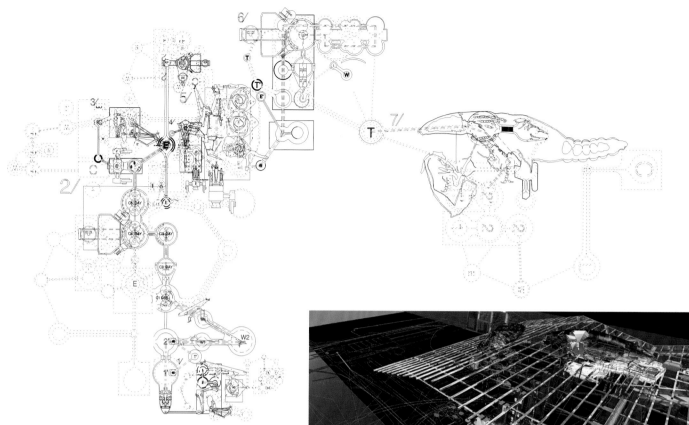

Plan showing the seven formalised laboratories
and the ways in which they interconnect to best
facilitate the cloning process.

Plan showing the scientific process in the larger context of the
other occupants of the building. The paths shown are of specialised
staff and potential parents, as well as specific moments at which
they interact with the path of the potential embryo.

The location of the cloning clinic within an
existing water-filled warehouse. The seawater
is utilised as a cooling agent for the
laboratories, and the red pipe tracks the path
of the embryo through the cloning machine.
Scale: 10 to the power of 1 metre.

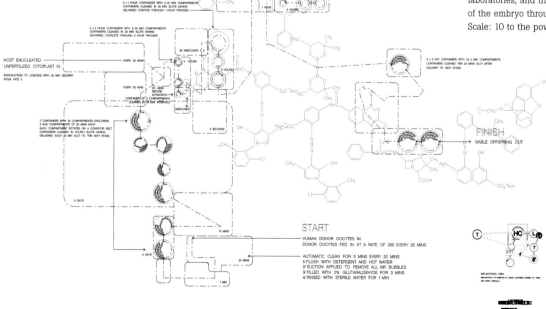

FINISH

VIABLE OFFSPRING OUT

HOST ENUCLEATED
UNFERTILIZED CYTOPLAST IN

INTRODUCTION TO COINCIDE WITH 20 MIN DELIVERY
FROM FATE 2

START

HUMAN DONOR OOCYTES IN
DONOR OOCYTES FED IN AT A RATE OF 300 EVERY 25 MINS

AUTOMATIC CLEAN FOR 5 MINS EVERY 20 MINS
1/ FLUSH WITH DETERGENT AND HOT WATER
2/ SUCTION APPLIED TO REMOVE ALL AIR BUBBLES
3/ FILLED WITH 2% GLUTARALDEHYDE FOR 3 MINS
4/ RINSED WITH STERILE WATER FOR 1 MIN

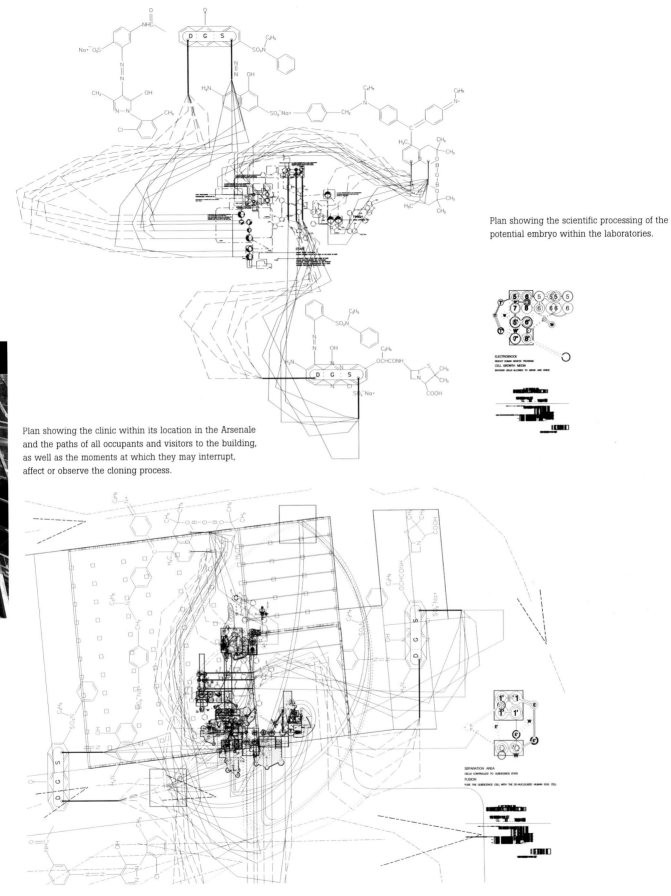

Plan showing the scientific processing of the potential embryo within the laboratories.

Plan showing the clinic within its location in the Arsenale and the paths of all occupants and visitors to the building, as well as the moments at which they may interrupt, affect or observe the cloning process.

Note

1. The Human Cloning Clinic project was developed in Unit 18 (Colin Fournier/Peter Szczepaniak) at the Bartlett School of Architecture, UCL, during 1998–99.

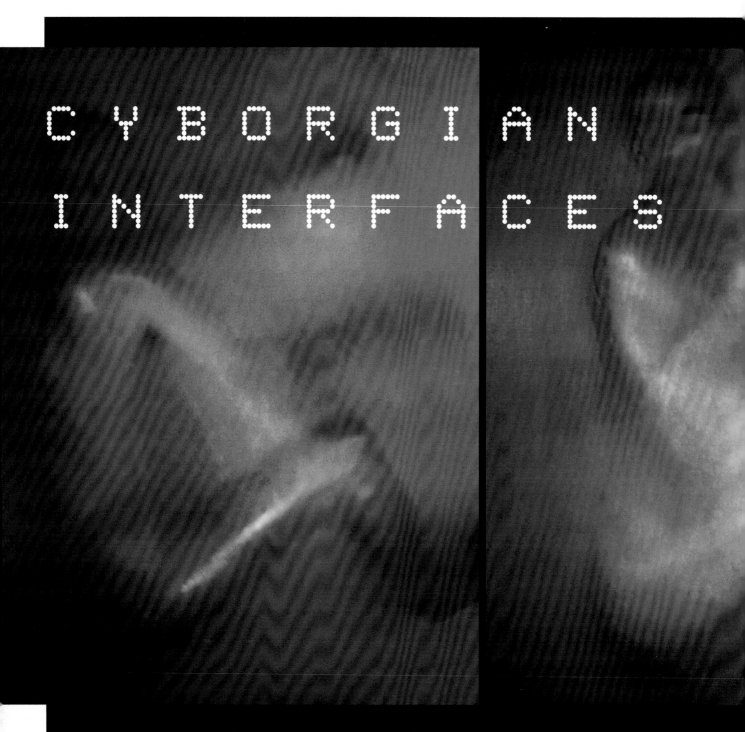

CYBORGIAN INTERFACES

A synthesis of organic and synthetic parts, the cyborg in film and fiction provides an important means in the digital age by which to question and explore the difference between human and artificial intelligence. As cyberspace becomes ever more pervasive, and invasive, and interfaces become softer, William J Mitchell's vision of plugging the individual's nervous system into electronic organs hastens. Here, **Marcos Cruz** breathes life into the cyborg in his Cyborgian Interfaces and In-Wall projects.

In the last 20 years, a lot has been said about our existential condition of being cyborgs, but very little has been designed that suggests how this cyborgianism is affecting our built environment. William Mitchell's famous argument that our human inhabitation is gaining a different meaning – 'one that has less to do with parking your bones in architecturally defined space and more with connecting your nervous system to nearby electronic organs. Your room and your home will become part of you, and you will become part of them'[1] – is still left unanswered in terms of design. In this sense, Cyborgian Interfaces[2] are a response to Mitchell's challenge, and feature a home for cyborgs[3] that goes beyond the traditional notions of dwelling. It is a place of hyperconnectivity[4] in which inhabitants step into their surrounding walls in order to spend most of the time in (virtual) communication with others. But these walls are more than walls; they are inhabitable interfaces explored via teletactility[5] that incorporate several service devices: Storage Capillaries, In-Wall Seats, Relaxing Cocoons, Communication Suits and Gestural Tentacles. In these wall interfaces, essential domestic functions such as sitting, sleeping or communicating are transferred from the traditional room space into the walls.

In material and constructive terms, Cyborgian Interfaces are hybrid structures in which biological systems are implanted in specific zones of the architecture. Bearing in mind the definition of 'synthetic neoplasms',[6] these parts could be considered neoplasmatic in as much as they are semi-living entities that evolve in a system of partial life, as Oron Catts and Ionat Zurr of SymbioticA would call it.[7] Each of the proposed service devices is composed of three variable layers, defined respectively as an outside protective layer, an in-between structural layer, and an inside sensitive layer. While protective and structural layers are built as a continuous entity, varying in each case in thickness and elasticity, the inside layer is differentiated in terms of material, technology and form in accordance with each programmatic requirement. Its structure is composed of an intelligent gelatinous membrane, which is reinforced in specific places by a tensegrity skeleton embedded within. Recent studies about viscous composites show that these materials develop infinite degrees of internal stability and coherence in reaction to the external pressures of human movement and weight. For the duration of action in the Communication Suit, for example, the inside layer increases and decreases levels of viscosity along the human body. In cases such as this, the stiffening that occurs makes the substance behave less like a liquid or gel and more like a sticky solid.

The service devices of Cyborgian Interfaces are equipped with different types of haptic technologies embedded in the walls: basic force feedback devices that work in two dimensions between user and screen, and exoskeletal devices that exert tactile pressure on the skin, allowing for a three-dimensional engagement of body in virtual space.

Marcos Cruz, In-Wall Creatures, 1998
Performance in a latex wall at the Bartlett School of Architecture, UCL. The inhabitation of such a pliable and visceral environment puts forward a new haptic relationship between the human body and architecture, testing the possibilities of 'living in', 'living in-between' and 'living along' walls.

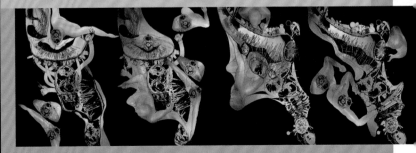

Marcos Cruz, In-Wall Creatures 1, 1999–2001
Plan: scale 1:2.5. Proposal of a neo-biological inhabitable environment in which biological and non-biological structures are hybridised.

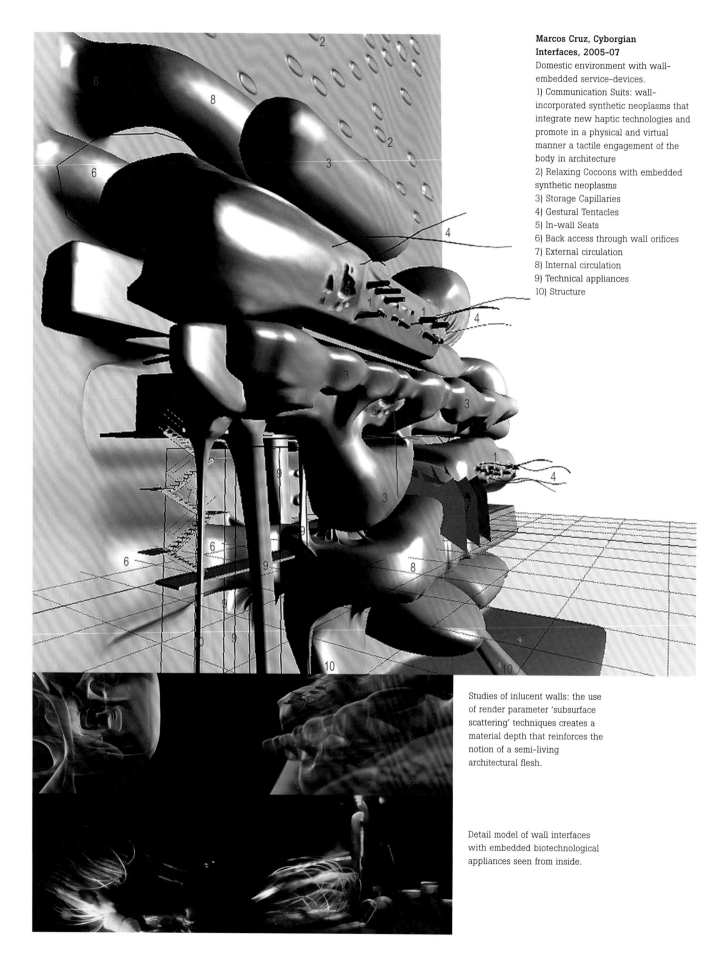

Marcos Cruz, Cyborgian Interfaces, 2005-07
Domestic environment with wall-embedded service-devices.
1) Communication Suits: wall-incorporated synthetic neoplasms that integrate new haptic technologies and promote in a physical and virtual manner a tactile engagement of the body in architecture
2) Relaxing Cocoons with embedded synthetic neoplasms
3) Storage Capillaries
4) Gestural Tentacles
5) In-wall Seats
6) Back access through wall orifices
7) External circulation
8) Internal circulation
9) Technical appliances
10) Structure

Studies of inlucent walls: the use of render parameter 'subsurface scattering' techniques creates a material depth that reinforces the notion of a semi-living architectural flesh.

Detail model of wall interfaces with embedded biotechnological appliances seen from inside.

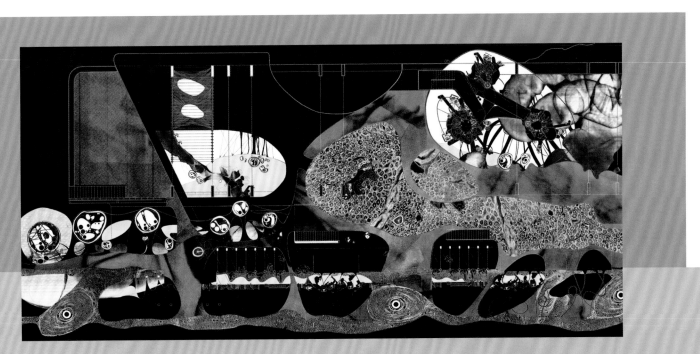

Marcos Cruz, Hyperdermis, 1999–2001
Plan: scale 1:25. Essential domestic functions such as sitting, sleeping or communicating are transferred into inhabitable wall interfaces that incorporate Storage Capillaries, In-Wall Seats, Relaxing Cocoons, Communication Suits and Gestural Tentacles.

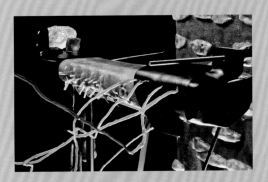

Marcos Cruz, Hyperdermis, 1999
Latex model with wall interfaces in which users engage in virtual communication via an 'exoskeletal skin' that is linked to the worldwide digital net. The 'skin' is a semi-biological apparatus that is embedded with hyper-technological equipment, such as data suits, sensor gloves and robotic prostheses.

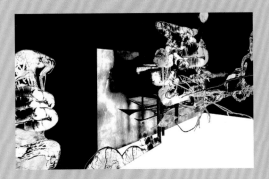

Marcos Cruz, Cyborgian Interfaces, 1999
Preliminary collages of Cyborgian Interfaces constructed with X-ray images of entrails and bone structures.

For Storage Capillaries and In-Wall Seats, computer-manufactured textiles such as micro-fibres are employed; that is, extremely fine and soft woven fabrics with crease-resistance and sheer appearance. Digital definition makes it possible to weave the micro-fibres densely enough to make them windproof, water resistant and breathable all at the same time. They are able to maintain a constant temperature in oscillations of hot and cold conditions. For the design of Relaxing Cocoons and Communication Suits, a different technology is required. As long-term inhabitable environments, these surfaces function as skin-sensitive and micro-textured surfaces, as well as enabling high degrees of hygienic care. Artificial skin is inserted in their interiors, a procedure that requires high levels of control and maintenance, and is monitored and kept alive via numerous small bioreactors that supply the skin with nutrients and regulate its environmental conditions. For Gestural Tentacles, 'shape memory polymers' are reinforced by an embedded prosthetic armature that is movable by artificial muscle fibres, enabling these extremities to move freely in space. ⟁

Notes
1. William J Mitchell, *City of Bits: Space, Place and the Infobahn*, MIT Press (Cambridge, MA), 1996, p 30.
2. Cyborgian Interfaces is a project developed by Marcos Cruz in the context of his Masters in Architectural Design 'Fleshscape' (tutors: Patrick Weber and Nikolaus Pamarsche) and PhD by Design 'The Inhabitable Flesh of Architecture' (supervisors Professor Peter Cook and Professor Jonathan Hill), undertaken at the Bartlett School of Architecture, UCL, between 1998–99 and 2000–07.
3. This expression is originally from Anthony Vidler's chapter 'Home for Cyborgs' in *The Architectural Uncanny: Essays in the Modern Unhomely*, MIT Press (Cambridge, MA), 1992, pp 147–64.
4. William J Mitchell, *ME++: The Cyborg Self and the Networked City*, MIT Press (Cambridge, MA), 2003, p 31.
5. Claudia Benthien talks about 'teletactility' – an expression originally used by the Norwegian media artist Stahl Stenslie – as a phenomenon that implies the merging of different sensory experiences in both human flesh and virtual perception. This entails a new spatio-mental dimension in which sensual experience of closeness and intimacy through touch becomes concurrent with physical distance and a sense of anonymity. See Benthien's chapter 12, 'Teletactility: The Skin in New Media', in Claudia Benthien, *Skin: On the Cultural Border Between Self and World*, Columbia University Press (New York), 2002, pp 221–34.
6. See 'Synthetic Neoplasms' on pp 36–43 of this issue.
7. The expressions 'semi-living' and 'partial life' were originally used by Oron Catts and Ionat Zurr of SymbioticA in the introduction to their Extra-Ear – 1/4 Scale project. See: www.tca.uwa.edu.au/extra/extra-ear.html.

Comfo-Veg Club

Peter Cook, Comfo-Veg Club, 2008

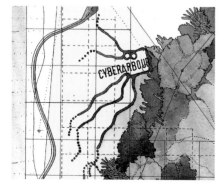

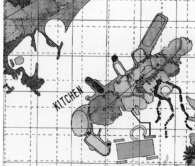

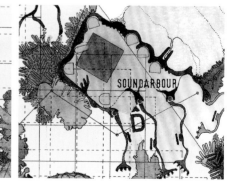

Peter Cook, Veg House Stage 2, 1996
Detail of cyberarbour.

Detail of kitchen.

Peter Cook, Veg House Stage 3, 1996
Detail of soundarbour.

Drawn expressly for this issue of *AD*, **Peter Cook's** Comfo-Veg Club builds on the biological theme and aesthetic of some of his earlier works. A garden and definitely 'green', the space is amorphous and ambiguous in every other way. Vegetative, it is soft, draping and melting, ever shifting in its spatial and material qualities.

The Comfo-Veg Club continues and expands some themes first introduced in the 1970s with the Sponge project and in the early 2000s with the Veg House and Veg Village. The 'club' is, in effect, a place where the idea of work place and pleasure-place symbolically and operationally melt. Where the definition of an activity only exists via a few clues and memories. Occasionally one spots a feature that is (reassuringly?) retained from the conventional office or club world: the operating console, the drinks cabinet, the 'lounger'.

A softly defined rectangular space acts as a frame for movies or information screens and also for the occasional densification of secret territory: but the 'screen' can melt too. The frame is perverted – or rather enhanced – by being a vegetated and changeable element. Suggestions of hard activity are constantly overlaid by the redefinition of form: everything can shift, change density, colour, smell, softness or hardness. Consoles and 'workstations' only pop up if needed. Much can be achieved while lying down or 'lolling' about. The ceiling is deliberately melted into a series of kite-like wafers and airshafts, plant-like leaves and drapes. As with the Veg House, all of these constantly shift and metamorphose between the territory of 'drape', 'vegetable', 'appliance', 'clothing', 'bedding', 'architecture'. Some of the drapes are decoys, some are privacy related. Members of the club can summon up more or less personal screening, more or less sound, more or less softness, more or less gadgetry.

Anyway, it is more of a garden than a large room.

Details to Note: A Deliberate Ambiguity About Origins of Parts
The furniture-ground is definitely mechanical – or is it?
The drapes are definitely lightweight – or are they?
The communication screens are definitely of a different ilk to the softer stuff – or are they?
The consoles are arguably 'devices' – or are they?
This picture could be any colour: the 'veg' is green (more or less) in order to reassure – since it may all be fake. Or some of it? And so on. *ᗡ*

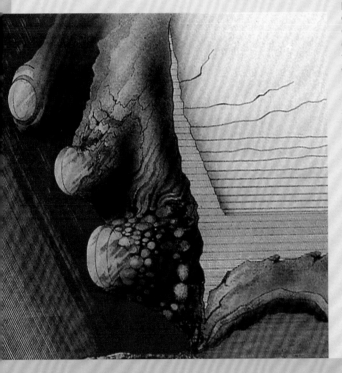

Peter Cook, Sponge, 1975
Orifices.

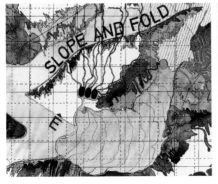

Peter Cook, Veg House Stage 4, 1996
Detail of slope and fold.

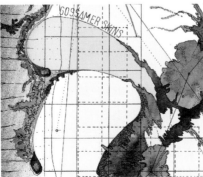

Detail of gossamer skins.

Detail of total conservatory.

Minimal Surface Geometry and the Green Paradigm

Sulan Kolatan introduces two projects by Kol/Mac – INVERSAbrane and MUTEN Galataport – that create a new biological or green paradigm through minimal surface geometry, reinterpreting and reinventing the notion of urban ecology, as defined topologically.

The interface between topology and urban ecology constitutes a productive inquiry in Kol/Mac's current work. Unlike traditional urban-design approaches, urban ecology does not distinguish between various urban typologies, but instead emphasises the continuity of urban surface and its systemic performances. It looks at the city as a vast contact surface configured by a multitude of contiguous patches. One could argue that it views the world topologically. Furthermore, it evaluates the performance of this surface with regard to materiality, density, capacity, colour and form, thus linking the quality of urban ecology to the specific qualities present in these categories. Taking this into account, Kol/Mac's design methods are built on linking computationally generated (smart) form with condition-based high performance.

INVERSAbrane[1] and MUTEN Galataport, two Kol/Mac projects of very different scales, are representative of this approach. Both deploy a combination of artificial intelligence and minimal surface geometry to create excessive and often complex contact surfaces in response to generic and specific conditions. The goal is to enhance the surfaces' contact with air, sun and water through characteristics such as an economy of the material-to-strength ratio, a maximisation of the surface-to-volume ratio, the inversability of the exterior surface and the complexity of surface curvature/incline that adhere to these geometries. Whether as a building membrane or as urban landscape, the flat, smooth, impervious and often dark qualities of existing urban surfaces create a pathological environmental effect on contact with the elements. In comparison, Kol/Mac's proposed surfaces are designed to collect and slow the speed of rainwater, absorb sun energy through maximum exposure, and circulate a maximum volume of air in order to clean it on contact. Structurally, the minimal surface is highly economical in that it affords strength through curvature and form instead of thickness of material (see, for example, Arup's evaluations of sample cells).

Kol/Mac, INVERSAbrane, 2006–07
Prototype study in 'flesh'.

Animation stills. Building with a generic curtain wall (first row, left) and with a sample INVERSAbrane (first row, right); Rainwater recycling (second row, left and right) and fresh-air supply (third row, left); Heads Up Display technology in glass indicates levels of air pollution before cleaning and clean air supply (third row, right); Solar energy absorption across surface during a 24-hour cycle (fourth row, left); Air supply valve (fourth row, right); and Air and water handling details (fifth row).

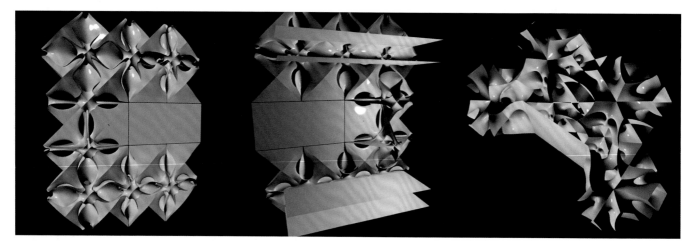

Kol/Mac, INVERSAbrane, 2006–07

Connection studies: transitions between minimal surface geometry and flat surfaces at 0 and 90 degrees. Left and middle: Window and slab connections (Generation 02). Right: Window connection (Generation 01).

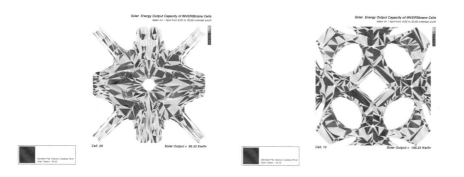

Solar output studies: quantification of solar energy capacity in relation to variable minimal surface geometry. The capacity of a same-size conventional/flat exterior panel is shown below for comparison.

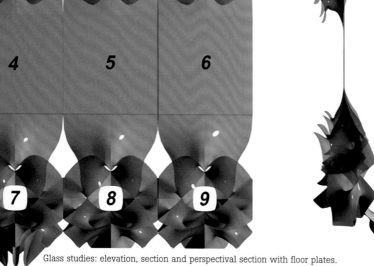

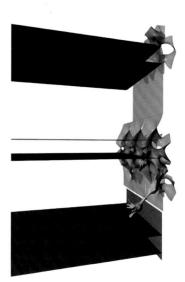

Glass studies: elevation, section and perspectival section with floor plates.

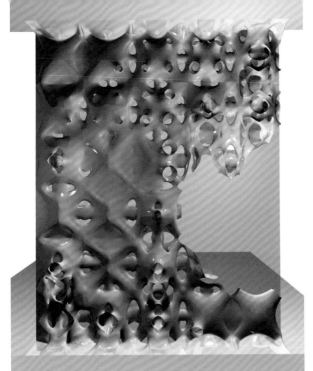

Prototype 1.0 (Generation 03; MoMA version, exhibited at 'SAFE: Design Takes On Risk', 2005.

Fenestration studies. Top: framing of windows with multiple-scale membrane cells. Bottom: clustering of cells and windows.

INVERSAbrane

INVERSAbrane focuses on going beyond the current 'green' curtain-wall standard through the strategic linking of advanced geometry, material and structural engineering, digital fabrication technologies and emerging expertise in ecology and biomedia. It is an exterior membrane and infrastructure, and its performance is based on excess surface, which maximises contact with the environment and creates a unique opportunity for eco-systemic exchanges between building and city. Air, water and light are recycled through it and used as sources of energy, and the membrane's capacity to invert links exterior and interior into a mutually enhancing feedback system to produce greater safety and comfort for both environments.

Rather than adopt a more common approach to safety based solely on bracing against a potential danger or reducing 'negative effects', INVERSAbrane aims to follow the kind of thinking that drives the design of racing cars and extreme-sports equipment. Here, increased safety allows for higher performance, and greater range and elevation of accepted standards. INVERSAbrane is extremely safe. It aims to enhance life rather than to merely preserve and increase performance in order to transform.

INVERSAbrane is seen as part of a natural evolution, one that connects the most fundamental design technologies with the most leading edge. With the increasing naturalisation of INVERSAbrane, two successive scenarios are projected. In the near term, INVERSAbrane is a high-performance building exterior, one that works like a racing car exterior or a firefighter's suit, and less like a common wall. In the longer term, INVERSAbrane is a living membrane, one that works more like a tree bark or an animal's skin. INVERSAbrane is a project in progress.

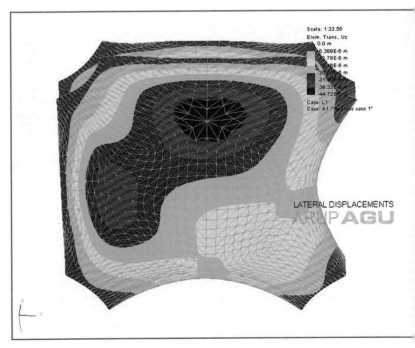

Structural studies on INVERSAbrane by Arup's Advanced Geometry Unit (AGU), London. Lateral displacement across the minimal surface of a sample cell.

MUTEN Galataport

The MUTEN Galataport proposal considers the entire urban surface as a continuum. There are no discrete separations between horizontal, vertical and inclined surfaces. Minimal surface geometry and surface topology are favoured over building typology. In order to test ranges of topology with regard to their capacity to affect the flow of water and wind as well as the absorption of solar energy, simulations are performed and the variations are organised according to a catalogue of similarities. Each variation constitutes a cell combining building, nature and infrastructure to varying degrees, sizes and shapes.

The parameters in this case include water as a heavily favoured programmatic element. As the remediation and clean-up of the Golden Horn, an inlet of the Bosphorus dividing the city of Istanbul and forming a natural harbour, is progressing, Kol/Mac is envisioning commercial, leisure and infrastructural uses that bring back historic activities to enliven the site and mix in new ways. The undercroft is partly permeated by seawater and partly by rainwater (two separate systems). While the coral-like complex surface creates an ideal habitat for sea life, and thus for activities ranging from urban aqua-farming to scuba diving, a separate system of scoops and chambers collects, filters and stores fresh rainwater in a vast underwater cistern. ◬

Note

1. INVERSAbrane is sponsored by Dupont Corian, Dupont Kevlar, Autodesk, Evans&Paul and BioGraphic Technologies, Inc.

Kol/Mac, MUTEN Galataport, Golden Horn, Istanbul, Turkey, 2006
Galataport perspectives. Top to bottom: view from street; one of the marinas; the building-to-landscape transition through minimal surface geometry; above/underground transitions at sea level.

Overall view. The existing urban patch consisting of a large concrete platform with warehouses is replaced by an urbanscape of minimal surface geometry. Due to its complex geometry, this new patch creates previously absent beneficial exchanges between its total urban surface and its environment.

Variable building/landscape cell topologies. These indicate a sample range generated by linking artifical intelligence software with minimal surface geometry. The underlying topological system is thus capable of adaptation to specific conditions. The limited range shown here displays the capacity of this design method to generate a wide array of implied typologies, from high-rise to institutional, to large spaces of assembly such as exhibition and concert halls, as well as arenas and malls.

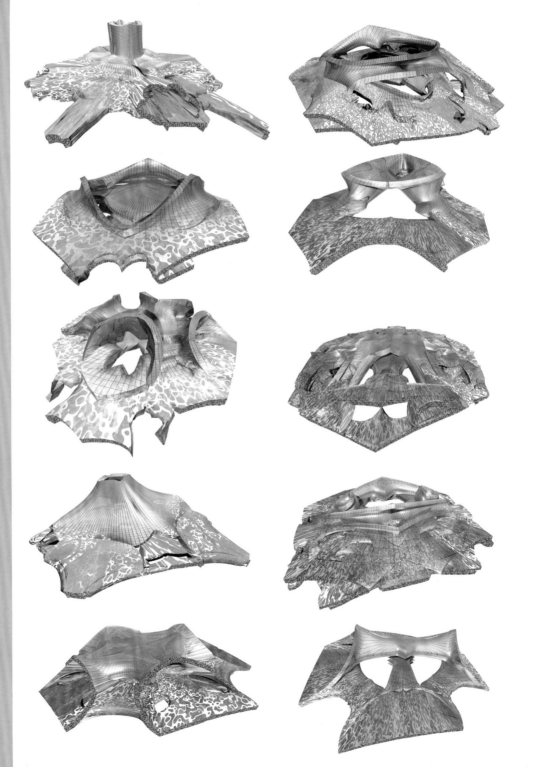

Bodies Without Organs – BwO

François Roche of R&Sie(n) advocates a means in which biological effects in architecture can go 'beyond the realm of physiological transfers'. Introducing new spatial relationships, they surpass being a mere '"green" alibi' and have the potential to transform architectural and urban space.

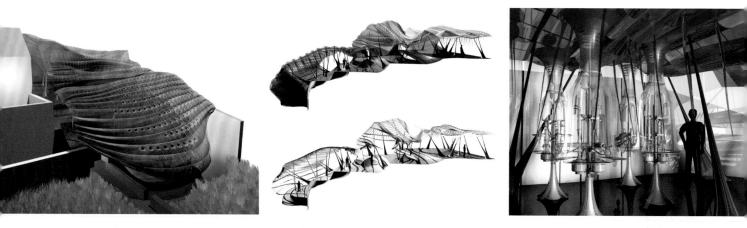

R&Sie(n), TheGardenofEarthlyDelights, Lopud, Croatia, 2008
In this greenhouse for alchemic experiments, medicinal plants, often used as poisons or antidotes in the Middle Ages around the Mediterranean region (especially in Franciscan monastery gardens), are employed in a top-down terraced morphology that suggests the emission of a toxic lava mass, creating the overall effect of a liquid-viscous greenhouse. 'Nasty' spikes are proposed to support a porous ETFE roof that irrigates the plants. Distillation, sublimation, extraction and drying machines are used for the metamorphosis of plants into juices, ointments and infusions.

R&Sie(n) with Benoît Durandin, Swarm-Town, Korea, 2006
The urban morphologies of this masterplan for an administrative town in Korea are generated by three generative scripts: 1) a flow script (as urban grid processes); 2) a ZXY scaler script (as urban density processes); and 3) a nerves script (as an urban indoor-outdoor interface).

Overall view of the masterplan in which the three scripted processes are applied: topographical relief (geography and topo-morphology of the location), shape (building emergences and volumetric skyline), and programme (as a rereading of the generative shape, by induction-deduction-reprogramming of the volumetric iterations results).

The emphasis that R&Sie(n), as a design studio, places on the physio-psychological takes the impact of biological effects beyond the realm of physiological transfers. It understands them also as a narrative system that introduces a type of heterotopian relationship with the body: *Bodies without Organs – BwO*, in the sense of Antonin Artaud and Gilles Deleuze.[1] It affords an apparatus that articulates substances and intensities, sliding surfaces and infiltration in a multitude of possibilities and interpretations. The *BwO* of R&Sie(n)'s projects are generated directly from the circumstance of production. They are embedded within the situational body as a graft, sharing viscera and viscosity without a clear identity that distinguishes its own individuality, its own emergences and the situation itself.

Several projects have been used to explore such scenarios. For example, Green Gorgon suggests the existence of a constructed phasmida, which feeds the confusion between artificial and domesticated nature, where all facades become a swamp of moist recycling parts that clean dirty water. TheGardenofEarthlyDelights, on the other hand, proposes a greenhouse in Croatia that incorporates a toxic garden. Yet this building can be tasted and tested through a distillation process only by voluntary desire, similar to the way that the fugu (Japanese puffer fish) physiologically and psychologically affects the metabolism of the guinea-pig participants who risk eating it. Olzweg is an unachieved labyrinth for the FRAC, Orléans, a primary museum of radical architecture where people can lose themselves and discover a heterotopian non-panoptical system of trajectories using a personal digital assistant (PDA) on a radio frequency identification (RFID) device to return to their own positions at XYZ, simultaneously developing strategies to move again. In Swarm-Town, an eco-software city proposed as a new urban plan in Korea, the challenge is to engage nature as the designer of the city: a 'terraforma' experiment. Through a pre-programmed and scripted process, variability and adaptability in the combination of topographical relief, shape and programme can be introduced. The *genius loci* is no longer a 'green' alibi, but rather a transformational vector of urbanism. ∆

Note

1. Antonin Artaud, 'Pas de bouche, pas de langue, pas de dents, pas de larynx, pas d'oesophage, pas d'estomac, pas de ventre, pas d'anus,' quoted by Gilles Deleuze and Felix Guattari in *L'Anti-Œdipe: capitalisme et schizophrénie*, Les Editions De Minuit (Paris), 1972.

R&Sie(n) with Philippe Parreno, Green Gorgon, Lausanne, Switzerland, 2005
The design of the museum relies on a series of key strategies: 1) to recognise the deceit of its natural environment (polder development on the lake); 2) to develop a heterotopia that is testicular, uncertain and organic; 3) to blur the boundaries between different understandings of 'nature', ie built natures (hydroponic facade, biodynamic green hairs) and urban, rather more spontaneous and 'haunted' natures, which altogether generate a hybrid, non-identifiable new landscape; 4) to use the photosynthesis of all green facades to recycle and clean wastewater; 5) to affect the morphology of internal exhibition spaces with the outer knotted geometry of the building; 6) to introduce an 'i-compass' system in which visitors navigate through the building with portable GPS systems that are coupled with an informational PDA.

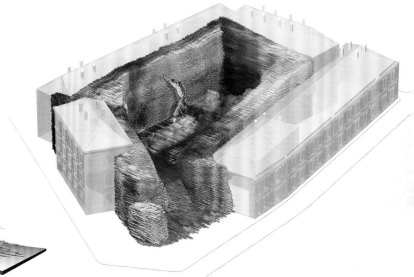

R&Sie(n) with Pierre Huyghe, Olzweg, FRAC, Orléans, France, 2006
A labyrinth of paths and walkways is embedded within this mass of scripted glass components, which are largely created from recycled waste glass.

The process of construction and cleansing is assisted by robots (with or without automatism) that enable a randomisation and uncertainty in the final shape, ultimately also allowing the reprogramming of the labyrinth during construction itself. The construction schedule is planned for a period of more than 10 years – an agglomeration of 'work to be done' that should be understood as a factor of desire with a desirable machine.

Uto-Purification

Yukihiko Sugawara envisions a new dynamic process for transforming derelict post-industrial sites into a fertile natural habitat. Human waste is applied sequentially and the indigenous ecosystem is reorganised as a catalyst for the newly verdant environment.

Yukihiko Sugawara, Uto-purification, 2003
Moulding Tubules. Sunlight passes through the layered bio-topic landscape.

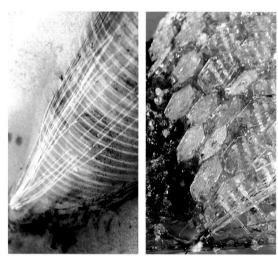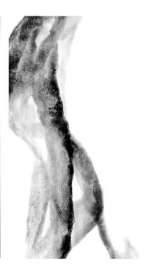

The Uto-purification apparatus: the Bulgy Oasis, Moulding Tubules, an Injection Tree, the Vege-Lung and the Bio-topia Hut.

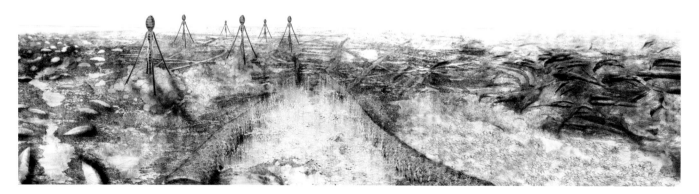

A verdant environment emerges, a bio-topic landscape induced by the Rhizo-diversification System. Dereliction and waste give way to a diverse, complex, self-organised ecosystem: the result of Uto-purification.

'Uto-purification' is an amalgamated term that merges the utopian with purification.[1] It intimates a new biological utopia embracing purification, fertilisation and recultivation. In order to induce the self-organised ecosystem that is required for Uto-purification on derelict land, bioreactors are employed as components of a Rhizo-diversification System. Each application of this system is relative to the particular context, the ultimate goal being Uto-purification. Organic waste is proposed as the main resource, fuelling an applied and enhanced natural process that regenerates derelict land, transforming it into a verdant environment.

Dereliction and organic waste are the results of excessive human activities and the negative impacts of our industrialised society. However, the Rhizo-diversification System uses both as precious resources. For example, derelict land provides the site of the 'Bio-topia', and the organic waste the valuable biomass that facilitates the transformative process. Thus Uto-purification has a complementary relationship with the human activities that produce organic waste and dereliction.

A sequential application of the process supports a sustainable treatment of the site, reorganising the indigenous ecosystem and giving rise to a new green frontier. This results in a bio-topian network: an ecosystem in which diverse assemblies of organisms inhabit a three-dimensionally laminated space, and are intrinsically related to their environment. The Rhizo-diversification System presents the catalyst for regeneration. Vegetation provides a medium by which archi-form and land-form seamlessly overlap and merge. Self-organisation establishes itself progressively and, with the proliferation of organic variety and complexity, a horticultural environment emerges that harnesses the natural ecosystem and embodies micro-organic mechanisms while engaging human activity. An opportunity for permaculture is thus presented, and with it the sustainable coexistence of flora and fauna. ⚙

Note

1. The Uto-purification project was developed in the Yamashita Lab under the guidance of Professor Hideyuki Yamashita at the Nagaoka Institute of Design – Department of Environmental Design, Japan, from 2000 to 2003.

Composition of A Cell of Reactor   Conversion of Substances   Water Flow in Reactor

Section and System Flow of Reactor

Moulding Tubules. The assembly of a reactor cell and the system flow of the reactor process.

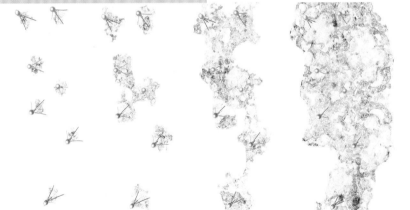

Injection Trees. The location for intervention is strategically plotted on the derelict site and the Rhizo-diversification System, with bioreactors, is installed. Gradual vegetation is induced, encouraging the fertile revitalisation of the site.

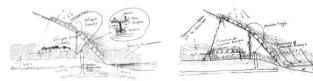

Phase1_Environmental Remediation Species   Phase2_ Environmental Remediation + Indigenous Species   Phase3_Indigenous + Horticultural Species   Phase Final_Indigenous Species

The environmental remediation phases. Indigenous species proliferate, and a horticultural environment emerges in which visitors occupy translucent rhizospheres and subterranean chambers composed of biodegradable plastics and laminated timber structures.

Algaetecture and Nonsterile

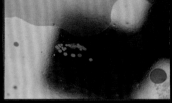

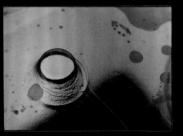

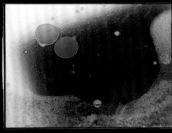

Steve Pike outlines a series of controlled experiments he embarked upon with microbiologist Conrad Mullineaux, which culminated in a final installation highlighting the potential of a microbiological-responsive architecture at a human scale. With these experiments, Pike challenges the way in which we commonly understand 'air' as a sterile and empty space, exploring the aesthetic implications of it as a mass of densely colonised matter that reflects users' activities via their bacteriological traces.

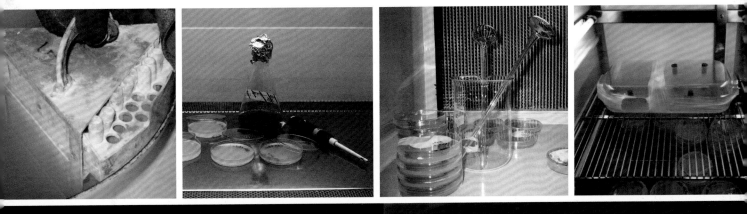

Steve Pike, Algaetecture, Interaction Vessel, 2001
opposite: Details of the preliminary Interaction Vessel. The device combines fabricated elements such as facilitator and inhibitor nodes, sporangiophores and the growth plane, with specific micro-organisms selected for their environmental requirements. In this instance, the cyanobacteria *Synechococcus* 7942 and *Fremyella diphosyphon* FD 7601 were employed for their vivid green appearance and their phototropic behaviour. These were introduced alongside the fungi *Alternaria brassicicola* and *Penicillium digitatum*, both utilising sporogenesis and airborne distribution to colonise the territory.

top: Preparation of the Interaction Vessel. Selecting the appropriate fungi, propagating the cyanobacteria, sterilisation of the vessel and sporangiophores, and the incubation of the assembled vessel.

bottom: The Interaction Vessel presented a controlled environment in which a degree of manipulation could be applied to the selected micro-organisms, while the less predictable situation of multiple colonial occupation could be observed. Metaphorical comparisons regarding issues of territorial conquest, encounter and negotiation are raised.

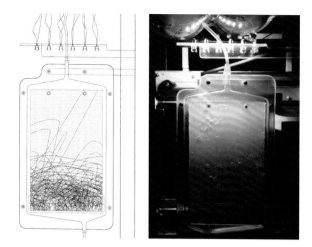

Algaetecture collectively embraces a series of studies, experiments and constructions that set out to explore micro-organic material and microbiological processes as prospective components and tools for design. The incorporation and application of microbial activity, its associated environmental modification capabilities and resultant material product, along with the extensive aesthetic considerations, offers immense potential for architecture. The knowledge and expertise of the microbiologist Professor Conrad Mullineaux was enlisted which, in collaboration with my intention as the designer, resulted in an interdisciplinary approach where the laboratory effectively became the design studio.

Initial investigations were concerned with the manipulation of small colonies of cyanobacteria, specifically photosensitive algae; the extent and form of their territorial progression was demonstratively controlled by withholding or applying light. These elementary studies progressed to the development of a series of Interaction Vessels, controlled environments in which differing micro-organisms were introduced and manipulated. By the application of facilitators and inhibitors, bespoke devices affording some influence over the microbial growth, the outcome could be partially designed with other parameters established by the self-determination of the colonies themselves. The facilitators applied point light sources for the phototropic cyanobacteria and more generally a glycerine solution for fuel and hydration. By contrast, the inhibitors delivered a fungal growth restrictor or a chlorine solution. Extending the interdisciplinary approach, Dr Richard Strange brought his expertise in mycology, Nick Callicott his knowledge of CAD/CAM manufacture and numerous craftspeople and technicians lent their skills in the production of blown glass, vacuum-formed acrylic and various precision components, each guided by the overall design intent.

Steve Pike, Algaetecture, Scanpad, 2001
The development of the Scanpad addressed two critically obstructive limitations of traditional microbiological practice in relation to the spatial considerations of architectural design. Firstly by introducing a reinforced vertical growth plane, presenting the ability to apply micro-organisms beyond the horizontal two dimensions, and secondly by integrating a flat-bed scanning device, facilitating the sequential monitoring of the resultant colonial progression.

Steve Pike, Algaetecture, Vitreous Interaction Vessel, 2001
The second version of the Interaction Vessel employed blown-glass fabrication techniques in its manufacture. CAD-generated data was not appropriate in this case, and the design intent was communicated exclusively by freehand sketches. The vessel was then crafted by Ian Hankey at the Royal College of Art, under guidance, in order to achieve the required proportion, chamber volume, input nodes and drainage spouts.

Reinterpreting the language and, to a degree, the function of laboratory equipment, the vitreous Interaction Vessel provided a contained, partially controlled environment to which moisture, heat, light source and nutrients could be applied and excessive condensation extracted.

Steve Pike, Algaetecture, Transformer Vessel and Monitor Vessel, 2001
Employing essentially similar apparatus, the Transformer Vessels and Monitor Vessels differ in one
fundamental aspect: the chemical design of the composition of the growth medium. The process of selecting
the type and proportion of the assembled chemicals, combining them, heating them in an autoclave and
setting the tailored growth medium within the vessel allows the deliberate propagation of specific micro-
organisms or the targeting of particular ambient microbial populations for monitoring.

Composition of BG11 for Synechocystis 6803

To make 1 litre of BG11 add the following stocks and autoclave:

X 100 Bg 11 stock	10 ml
Trace elements	1 ml
Iron stock	1 ml
Phosphate stock	1 ml
$Na_2 CO_3$ stock	1 ml
TES buffer	10 ml
Sodium Thiosulphate (solid)	3 g
1M $NaHCO_2$	10 ml

Rinse all glassware before use. Add filter-sterilised glucose (from 2M stock, to 5mM) if needed.

Stock solutions made as follows:

1 litre of x 100 Bg11 stock

$NaNO_3$	149.6 g
$MgSO_4.7H_2O$	7.49 g
$CaCl_2$	3.60 g
Citric acid	0.60 g
Na_2EDTA	1.12 ml of 0.25M solution @pH 8.0

100 ml of trace elements

H_3BO_3	0.286 g
$MnCl_2 4H_2O$	0.181 g
$ZnSO_4 7H_2O$	0.022 g
$Na_2MoO_4 2H_2O$	0.039 g
$Co(NO_3)_2 6H_2O$	0.005 g
$CuSO_4 5H_2O$	0.008 g

100 ml of iron stock

0.6 g of ferric citrate or 1.11 g of ferric ammonium citrate

100 ml of phosphate stock

3.05 g of $K_2 HPO_4$

100ml of $Na_2 CO_3$

2.0 g of $Na_2 CO_3$

TES Buffer

22.9 g of TES @pH 8.2

Agar:
Make double strength BG11 and 3% agar, then mix before pouring plates.

Growth:
Cells in liquid culture are grown shaking (not overly fast) @ 30ºc.
Plates grown in illuminated incubator @ 30ºc
(put beaker of dH_2O in incubator to maintain humidity)

Autoclave:
@ 121ºc for 15 mins.

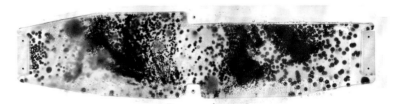

The Transformer Vessel displaying its distinctive
green field of cyanobacteria, or the Monitor Vessel
presenting the less predictable harnessed microbial
colonisation, are determined by the growth medium
they employ. The medium comprises a complex
chemical combination, which differs subject to the
design intent and is demonstrated by the tabular
description of the composition of the BG11 medium
tailored for *Synechocystis* 6803.

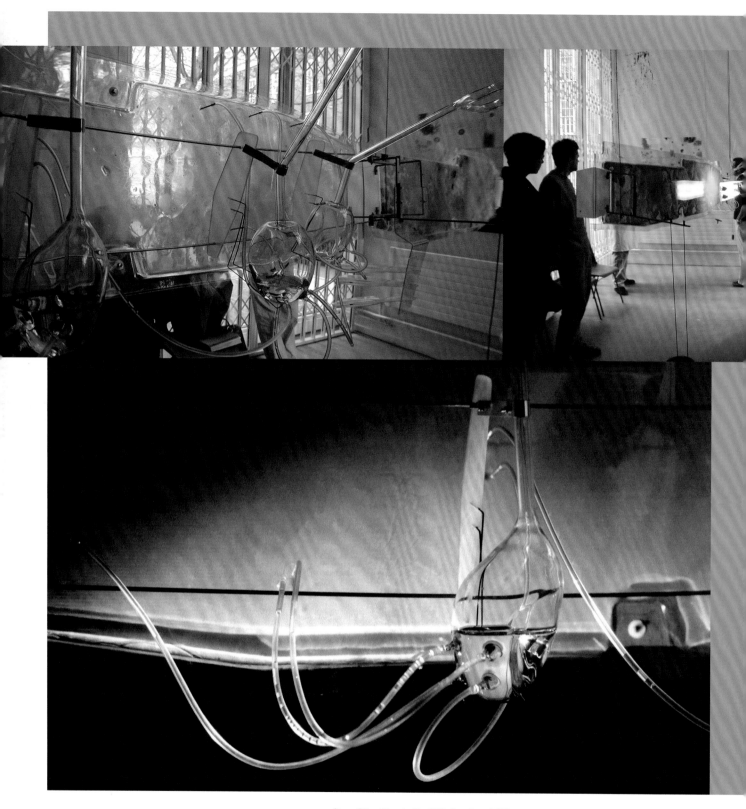

Steve Pike, Nonsterile, UCL, London, 2001

top: A suspended assembly of Monitor Vessels and a single Transformer Vessel, with associated support infrastructure, occupies, modifies and monitors its immediate environment.

bottom: A facilitator component, providing hydration, attached to a Monitor Vessel at the start of its exposure. Any captured ambient microbes have yet to display their presence.

In order for these investigations to yield any architectural potential, the limitations of the laboratory had to be addressed. The development of the Scanpad set out to test two paramount considerations: controlled growth across a vertical surface and the ability to monitor the resultant progression. A perforated membrane was set within a suitable growth medium and suspended within an enclosed acrylic vessel to provide a vertical plane. An arrayed light source was located at the top of the plane, with the distinctly phototaxic microbe *Synechococcus motile* introduced at the base. A planar scanning device was attached to the vessel, enabling periodic monitoring of the resulting emergent colony.

The information gathered and principles established by these studies were combined in the development of a final installation, which in addition addressed the issue of human scale. Transformer Vessels were constructed at half scale, each to a length of 1,200 millimetres (47.2 inches) – a considerable departure from the laboratory scale of the 90-millimetre (3.5-inch) diameter standard Petri dish. Designed as an architectural component, the vessels proposed that the inherent ability of certain algae to absorb CO_2 and to produce oxygen could be harnessed within an architectural surface, potentially modifying their immediate environment. They were created by heat-deforming, high-impact transparent acrylic, a resilient material readily sterilised; a taut nylon membrane was suspended and set within an agar-based growth medium incorporating the cyanobacteria *Synechocystis* for uniform growth. A partially living hybrid emerged, with the vessels assembled alongside the requisite support infrastructure of facilitators, inhibitors, structure and discharge systems.

Maintaining sterile conditions became a predominant concern of the installation. Inevitably, contamination occurred as ambient micro-organisms infiltrated the vessels, subverting the transformative intent. In response, a compositional modification transpired and the Nonsterile installation emerged. The vessels were reconfigured to encourage the growth of captured microbes, and became Monitor Vessels. Filled with potato dextrose agar, a medium that facilitates fungal growth, contamination flourished, manifesting the imperceptible abundant cohabitants of the environment in which we exist. ∆

Note

The research and development for Algaetecture and the creation of Nonsterile embraced a distinct interdisciplinary process. Marcos Cruz and Salvador Perez Arroyo, in their capacity as tutors of Unit 20 at the Bartlett School of Architecture, UCL, proved invaluable. Professor Conrad Mullineaux and his staff at UCL's Department of Microbiology provided expertise and considerable assistance, along with the laboratory and associated equipment that effectively became the design studio. Dr Richard Strange of the UCL Department of Mycology offered his expert knowledge. Abi Abdolwahabi and Bim Burton at the Bartlett workshop provided considerable technical assistance. Nick Callicott lent notable CAD/CAM support and expertise. Ian Hankey of the Royal College of Art provided craftsmanship and facilities with regard to blown-glass fabrication.

Nonsterile was shown in London, Coimbra and Munich, with each installation exhibiting differing resultant colonisations, displaying the specific environmental conditions and disclosing the preceding activity and behaviour of the visiting public.

Steve Pike, Nonsterile, Architekturgalerie, Munich, Germany, 2003
The resultant displayed colonisations reveal the specific ambient microbial populations, to an extent disclosing the preceding activity and behaviour of the visiting public.

A partially living hybrid emerged, with the vessels assembled alongside the requisite support infrastructure of facilitators, inhibitors, structure and discharge systems.

Living Buildings

Make Architects and Max Fordham Consulting Engineers, Algae Tower, 2007–
Sectional visualisation through the building perimeter. The algae absorb CO_2 during sunlight hours. They are collected, filtered, harvested and placed in a bioreactor that generates biodiesel and biogas, as well as other biomass products.

Plants and buildings may not naturally assimilate, but as **Bill Watts** of Max Fordham Consulting Engineers and **Sean Affleck** of Make Architects explain there are many benefits to their integration. Here they describe the two projects that they are collaborating on – Algae Tower, and Thorpe Park in Leeds – that harness the positives of vegetative growth.

Plants and buildings traditionally do not get on: static, man-made spaces resist the vigour of growing things. But plants can do many things for us. They photosynthesise, turning solar energy into chemical energy, and transpire using water to cool themselves. Increased cooling is needed as summers get hotter, and building surfaces become hotter than the air, contributing to the overheating of our cities. However, due to evaporation a leaf can be lower in temperature than the air, thus planting the walls of our city 'canyons' would provide cooler air for streets and buildings. The large, porous surfaces of plants enable them to filter the air, removing particulates. Soft plant matter also provides acoustic absorption. With cooler, quieter, less polluted streets, we can stop sealing buildings and start opening windows.

The product of photosynthesis, pure oils could be used for food, fuel or feedstock for industries. Vertical farms have been suggested for New York as a way of reducing the energy needed to transport fresh food to consumers. The higher concentration of CO_2 produced by inhabitants will increase the photosynthesis production rate of plants. Single-celled algae can achieve a 20 per cent rate of energy transfer from sunlight, which is comparable to the best photovoltaic cells now available. If buildings were used to meet more of our food and energy needs, some of the land now needed for cultivation could be left for nature and recreation.

For the future, one can imagine using plants not just to clad buildings, but to create the whole structure. Root systems fix to the ground more effectively than concrete; trees tend to survive earthquakes. We can grow elements off site as with any prefabricated construction. Previously we have cultivated living species to suit our needs, and now we are acquiring tools to select and mix aspects of living systems. These engineered products are part of the biological carbon cycle; they are created using solar energy and decompose into the soil when useless. The living world can provide for most of our needs, from sewage disposal to data processing. We only need harness it.

Bill Watts

Architectural Integration of Plant Life

It is easy to sound as if you have strayed into the realms of science fiction when discussing living building systems, but Make Architects, in collaboration with Max Fordham Consulting Engineers, are currently working on two separate projects that seek to harness the power of plant life in this way.

The first of these is at Thorpe Park in Leeds, a business park of commercial offices featuring pavilions whose external walls support densely planted, living greenery that is an integral part of each building's environmental system. In place of a conventional chilled beam system, this system passes the cooling agent (water) through a series of externally mounted panels that are permanently moistened by rainwater run-off in order to facilitate the highly efficient process of evaporative cooling. The combination of warmth and dampness created by the evaporative cooling process also creates the perfect environment for plant life, which is supported within a special panel fixed to the exterior of the evaporative cooling array. Irrigated by nutrient-enhanced rainwater, these plants optimise the efficiency of the cooling process by increasing the overall area of the evaporative cooling surface as they grow. Such vertical fields could also be harvested several times a year, with the resulting matter fed into an anaerobic digester to produce a biogas that could be used to power the building.

The second project, for an experimental Algae Tower, explores how architecture can integrate an even more efficient form of plant life with a host of applications. Algae are 200 per cent more effective at absorbing CO_2 than conventional corn crops and do not drain natural resources to the same degree. They also grow at an exponential rate and can be harvested almost every hour to produce not only biofuels, but also nutrients for livestock feed and even cosmetics. Accordingly, this project proposes a building that is wrapped in a series of tubes containing an algae suspension. The tubes are integrated into the cladding system so that they help insulate and shade interior spaces; in return, they absorb both the heat generated by the building and the sunlight that falls on them to create the perfect living conditions for algae, which are then collected, filtered and processed to generate biofuel to power the building as well as other biomass products. The algae also have the potential to bring a fascinating element of colour and texture to the structure's facade, producing an elevation that changes colour according to the lifecycle of the algae living within it: a perfect illustration of a dynamic and productive interface between nature and the built environment. ⌂

Sean Affleck

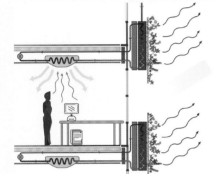

Make Architects and Max Fordham Consulting Engineers, Thorpe Park, Leeds, 2006–
Make's proposal utilises an external wall supporting densely packed living greenery. This planting is not purely for aesthetic purposes; it is also an integral part of the building's environmental system employing solar shading and evaporative cooling.

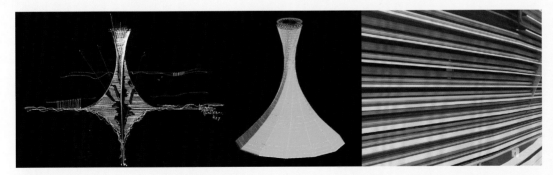

Make Architects and Max Fordham Consulting Engineers, Algae Tower, 2007–
The experimental project proposes a vision of buildings as cities, but also as power plants, absorbing CO_2 and producing biofuel. Employing walls as vertical fields for fuel crops, a suspension of algae contained within tubes envelops the external facade.

Algae occupy a series of tubes that wrap around the proposed building. Different species of algae result in differing wall colours, with some exhibiting bioluminescence.

Wonderwall

VenhoevenCS, Sportplaza Mercator, Amsterdam, 2006
The south elevation of the Sportplaza seen from the main outdoor swimming pool.

As the Wonderwall evolves, Rembrandtpark and Sportplaza Mercator merge together.

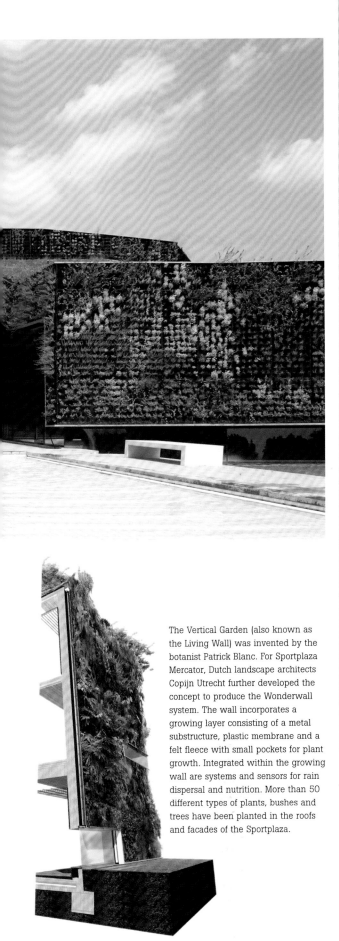

A lush, verdant mass of vegetation, the Sportplaza Mercator in Amsterdam by Venhoeven Architekten is an integral part of the environment, changing with the seasons.

Ton Venhoeven describes how landscape architects Copijn Utrecht's development of the Wonderwall system enabled him to realise his design for this growing structure.

Camouflaged Fortress

Sportplaza Mercator is a multifunctional sports complex built as a camouflaged fortress next to the entrance of the city of Amsterdam. Both roof and elevations are covered with 50 different species of plant, varying from lady's mantle to trees such as willow and birch. Over the years this will develop into wild and lush vegetation. The appearance of the building will alter over time and with every season. Like a ray it will be hardly visible from above and become an integral part of the environment. However, seen from ground level it reveals an exciting underworld with swimming pools, gymnasiums, and a party centre, aerobics studio and cafeteria.

Green Facade

Growing plants on more or less vertical elevations is complicated, thus landscape architects Copijn Utrecht developed the 'Wonderwall' system, an additional cladding on a waterproof elevation, specially for this purpose. The support structure of this second skin is made of steel beams that are connected to the building at the foundation and roof levels using specially designed synthetic-fibre blocks to prevent thermal bridges. Corrugated sheet metal supports the prefabricated panels of the Wonderwall system, which is made of synthetic fibre panels consisting of three different layers of ultraviolet-proof textile and foil. The inner layer is growth suppressing, the middle layer contains moisture, and the outer layer incorporates slits for the plants. The different layers are connected using staples. Once the various panels have been mounted, a balanced irrigation and feeding system is added. In this infrastructural system, plants are inserted on site.

The Dutch climate, the vertical position of the Wonderwall and the orientation of the differing parts of the building, with their varying exposures to sun and wind, create very specific biospheres. Thus in order to guarantee a lush vegetation on all elevations under such diverse circumstances, a specific assortment of plants was chosen for each orientation, and carefully arranged in grouped patterns to create a wild and varied camouflage. ⌂

The Vertical Garden (also known as the Living Wall) was invented by the botanist Patrick Blanc. For Sportplaza Mercator, Dutch landscape architects Copijn Utrecht further developed the concept to produce the Wonderwall system. The wall incorporates a growing layer consisting of a metal substructure, plastic membrane and a felt fleece with small pockets for plant growth. Integrated within the growing wall are systems and sensors for rain dispersal and nutrition. More than 50 different types of plants, bushes and trees have been planted in the roofs and facades of the Sportplaza.

Detail of the south facade. The variety of plant species gradually turns the building into a natural object, abundant with seasonal growth.

Artificial Evolution

A Hands-Off Approach for Architects

Rachel Armstrong highlights how developments in molecular biology and genetics are providing architects with insights into the properties of living matter, which are set to revolutionise design through the genesis of artificially evolving architectures.

HM Jonkers, Self-healing concrete – wall tests, TU Delft, The Netherlands, 2007
In this research project, the suitability of very specific but otherwise harmless bacteria are tested for their ability to repair cracks and thus significantly improve the durability of concrete structures. Such a bacterial repair mechanism would be beneficial for the economy and the environment at the same time, as concrete is, worldwide, the most applied building material. This new type of 'bio-concrete' would make costly manual repair work unnecessary and would minimise the use of raw materials, as structures would last much longer.

John M Johansen and Mohamad Alkayer, The Molecular House, 2000
The images represent a diary created by the owner of a molecular-engineered house written during its construction. The project is set in the year 2200.

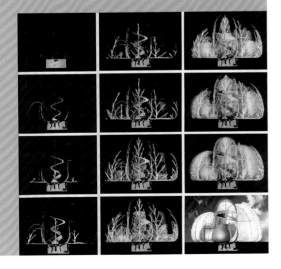

An ideal architecture is one that you can plant as a seed having programmed it with all the information it needs to grow itself in an environment where it can organically seek out and connect with the resources that it needs. Through its lifetime it would remain responsive to its surroundings and adjust according to the demands and needs of its human habitants. The architecture would be able to reproduce by cloning itself using a germ line structure that offers humans an opportunity to make any necessary genetic adjustments. The end of the lifecycle of the architecture would come when it is no longer responsive to human activity and becomes an inert, skeletal structure, possibly decaying into the ecosystem to be recycled by its progeny.

The Molecular House by American architects John M Johansen and Mohamad Alkayer operates on these design principles, which have been derived from the properties of plants, yet the qualities on which this autonomous architecture has been imagined do not belong exclusively to the plant kingdom.[1]

Life on this planet is about 4 billion years old, and natural systems have mastered strategies of growth, differentiation, complexity and evolution into locally specialised forms. Architects have already looked to biology for inspiration through the study of biomimetics, fascinated by the complex and variable properties of living systems, their programmability through genetic codes, responsiveness to the environment, and their ability to change over time. Recent discoveries at the molecular level suggest that it is possible to transgress the conventions of biological design, raising the possibility of manufactured living forms, and in so doing bring new processes, possibilities and organisms into the architectural domain. For example, the astrobiologist Paul Davies argues that using new molecular sequencing techniques, modern cells can be understood from molecular fossils that lie within them.[2] These findings may have implications for our understanding of the origins of 'higher' organisms that appear to have evolved as the result of collaboration between more primitive entities to survive the hostile conditions during the Archean period.

Unlike those fossils unearthed through traditional archaeological methods, these cytoplasmic fossils are living and functional within the modern cell, and although increasingly more vestigial members of the cell cytoplasm are being discovered through new methods of analysis, the active fossils are vital organelles such as mitochondria (symbiotic bacteria), tubulin (an ancient bacterial energy-producing molecule that forms the cellular skeleton) and peroxisomes (vesicles that protect against oxidation) that work in collaboration with the nucleic acid sequences of RNA and DNA to maintain cellular homeostasis.

Like the Archaea and symbiotic primitive bacteria before them, the tiny 'machines' and 'devices' that constitute nanotechnology may be regarded as potential symbiotic partners that may become an integral part of the organism. This symbiosis, however, would not be a random event like the arbitrary, wasteful processes described in 'natural selection', but a refined and deliberate relationship that is forced to occur by human intervention.

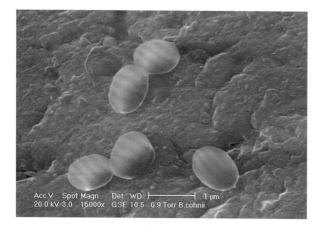

HM Jonkers, Self-healing concrete with Extremophiles, 2007
In nature, a huge number of different varieties of bacteria occur and some of these are likely to be well adapted to artificial man-made environments such as concrete. A specialised group of bacteria, the 'extremophiles', are not only known to love extremely dry and rock-solid conditions as in concrete, but also to be able to produce copious amounts of limestone. This calcium carbonate-based material, as well as other types of bio-minerals produced by bacteria, could serve to seal or heal cracks in concrete. The major goal of this research project is therefore to find the right bacteria, which can, when integrated in concrete, actively repair a structure during its 50- to 100-year service life.

Peter Cook and Colin Fournier, Kunsthaus Graz, Austria, 2003
Preliminary latex model of competition stage with pliable 'skin' and roof nozzles.

Suzanne Lee, BioCouture, London, 2007
This research project aims to address ecological and sustainability issues around fashion. It harnesses nature to propose a radical future fashion vision, investigating the use of bacterial cellulose, grown in a laboratory, to produce clothing. BioCouture was supported by Dr David Hepworth, co-director of CelluComp Ltd, and funded by a grant from the Arts and Humanities Research Council.

The lack of differentiation between animate and artificial at the molecular level has made materials science a lot more interesting. HM Jonkers from the Technical University, Delft, is already carrying out experiments with concrete that can heal itself with the help of bacteria, and can be used in 'growing' buildings. And with the integration of sensate technologies, architectures will not only be able to change with time; they will become responsive to their environment.[3]

The synthetic membranous roof of the elegant, globular glass-panel-clad Kunsthaus Graz in Austria, designed by Peter Cook and Colin Fournier, has been bestowed with sentient properties. This fossil-like structure was originally conceived as a biotechnologically constructed apparatus in which the roof was thought of as a technologised, touch-sensitive skin that hosted all secondary functions of the building, which in turn was punctuated with autonomously extendable, mobile nozzles that moved in response to microclimatic changes. This membrane also provided a dynamic interface with the environment through the activation of media cells that could be choreographed using varying degrees of opacity, translucency and transparency.[4] Indeed, architects are already taking a new approach to architectural practice based on the interrelationship of emergence and self-organisation concepts where architectural structures are not generated as singular and fixed bodies, but as complex energy and material systems that have a lifespan, and exist as part of the environment of other active systems, and as an iteration of a series that proceeds by evolutionary development.[5]

In the near future it may even be possible to consider certain forms of architecture as being 'alive'. In the 21st century, biologists are being forced to reimagine what constituted living processes through developments in the field and laboratory. Ground-breaking work by Hanczyc, Ikegami and colleagues constitutes the creation of an artificial protocell that resembles a living organism. This entity is not only capable of movement, but also of primitive 'sensation', and is all the more surprising having been generated entirely from inert material brought to 'life' in a test tube.[6] J Craig Venter has created the most controversy in this field by stripping down a whole living organism and removing everything that does not contain the components of interest, representing a significant experiment in biological minimalism.[7] Even more recently, in January 2008, Venter reversed this process and assembled nucleic acid building blocks to create the world's first artificially designed organism – *Mycoplasma laboratorium*[8] – an astonishing particle that is currently awaiting the final stage of its animation in the cell matrix of an enucleated host organism.

At Massachusetts General Hospital, researchers have constructed functional liver tissue from layers of tissue cells that are supported with biologically compatible scaffolding that encourages an autonomous blood supply;[9] and Professor Samuel I Stupp at Northwestern University in Illinois is using synthetic molecules to engineer artificially produced bone.[10]

With Biojewellery, designers Tobie Kerridge, Nikki Stott at the Royal College of Art and Ian Thompson of King's College London are already putting this 'bioavailable' material to use in making living bone jewellery fashioned for couples who agreed to wear rings made from their partner's bone cells. The cells were harvested from their wisdom teeth and jawbone, and then grown on a biocompatible scaffold, outside the context of a body.[11]

Other designers are exploring the potential of autonomously produced biomaterials. For example, in her BioCouture project, in collaboration with materials scientist David Hepworth, Suzanne Lee is making new fabric out of bacteria that make raw cellulose, a papyrus-like material, when they are cultured in sugared tea, and fashioning the product into garments that have a fragile skin-like appearance.[12]

Although the creation of an artificial genome is a landmark step in synthetic evolution, autonomous architectures are more likely to emerge using the inclusive collective principles of organisation exhibited by the cell cytoplasm, which will be regarded as the primary material of evolutionary change. New emergent relationships and identities will exist at this intimate level that will rival the alleged uniqueness of animate matter and challenge our definitions of life. Synthetic materials will exhibit molecular connectedness with networks, which, in turn, have the potential to make intimate connections with living systems. They will become part of us. ◬

Notes

1. See http://www.ona.vg/vision/growthhouse.html.
2. Paul Davies, in *The Origin of Life*, Penguin Books, 1999, p 56.
3. HM Jonkers, 'Self healing concrete: A biological approach', in *Self Healing Materials*, Springer Series in *Materials Design*, Vol 100, Springer Netherlands, 2007.
4. Information gathered from Marcos Cruz, member of the Kunsthaus competition team with Peter Cook, Colin Fournier, Niels Jonkhans and Mathis Osterhage, April 2008.
5. See Michael Hensel, Achim Menges and Michael Weinstock, *Techniques and Technologies in Morphogenetic Design*, AD, Vol 76, No 2, March/April 2006.
6. MM Hanczyc, T Toyota, T Ikegami, N Packard and T Sugawara, 'Fatty acid chemistry at the oil–water interface: self-propelled oil droplets', *J Am Chem Soc*. 129(30):9386–91, 2007.
7. For more on J Craig Venter's Synthesis of an Artificial Genome, see http://www.edge.org/3rd_culture/venter.boot07/venter.boot07_index.html.
8. Clyde A Hutchinson III, Scott N Peterson, Steven R Gill, Robin T Cline, Owen White, Claire M Frazer, Hamilton O Smith and J Craig Venter, 'Global transposon mutagenesis and a minimal mycoplasma genome', in *Science*, Vol 286, No 5447, 1999, pp 2165–9.
9. See 'A New Approach to Develop a Biohybrid Artificial Liver Using a Tightly Regulated Human Hepatocyte Cell Line', at http://sciencelinks.jp/j-east/article/200119/000020011901A0457975.php.
10. For more about Samuel I Stupp's genesis of artificial bone, see www.lib.bioinfo.pl/auth:Stupp,SI.
11. For more about Tobie Kerridge's Biojewellery, see http://www.biojewellery.com/.
12. Suzanne Lee, *Fashioning the Future: Tomorrow's Wardrobe*, Thames & Hudson (London), 2005.

Text © 2008 John Wiley & Sons Ltd. Images: pp 82, 84(t) © HM Jonkers; p 83 © John M Johansen for Concept & Design. Animation Mohamed Al Khayer; p 84(c) © model Marcos Cruz, photo Wanda Yu-Ying Hu and Steve Pike; p 84(b) © Suzanne Lee, photo Gary Wallis; p 85 © Tobie Kerridge

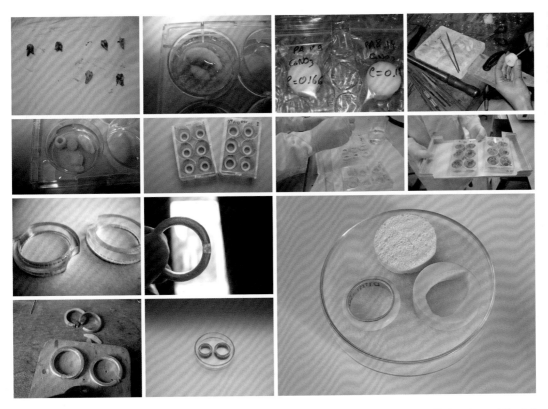

Tobie Kerridge with Ian Thompson, Biojewellery, London, 2005–06

1st row: Designing rings with bioengineered bone tissue. Left to right: Donated teeth; Growth of bone tissue in vitro; Synthetic polymer to be used as a scaffold; Preparation of the bioactive scaffold in a ring shape.

2nd row: The Biojewellery project began by looking for couples who wanted to donate their bone cells. Their cells were seeded on to a bioactive scaffold, a material that encouraged the cells to divide and grow rapidly. The resulting tissue took on the form of the scaffold, which was a ring shape. The couples' cells were grown at Guy's Hospital in London.

3rd and 4th row: The final bone tissue was taken to a studio at the Royal College of Art to be combined with traditional precious metals and made into a pair of rings for the couple, so that each of them has a ring made with the tissue of their partner.

above: Funding was awarded by the Engineering and Physical Sciences Research Council (EPSRC) as a part of its Partnership for Public Engagement initiative. The project led to a live debate at the Science Museum's Dana Centre in January 2006, and an exhibition at Guy's Hospital in London from December 2006, which included the rings and extensive documentary photos of the project.

Designer Materials for Architecture

The advent of nanotechnology enables us to scrutinise biological particles and processes at a scale never realised before. **Rachel Armstrong** looks at nanoparticles' relationship to biological processes and the subsequent implications for the development of new responsive materials for architectural design.

Anders Christiansen, Homeostatic Membrane, 2008
Homeostasis is the physiological process by which the internal system of architecture (humidity, temperature, acid–base balance) is maintained at equilibrium, despite variations in the external conditions. The homeostatic membrane acts as the overlap between the external conditions and internal requirements of a building. Drawing on current research in the fields of bioengineering and nanotechnology, it hosts a biosynthetic ecology of biological matter and technological mechanisms. This includes vessels of biological matter, flexible tissue, vent corridors, dynamic probes and a 'vascular' system connecting the vessels, along with a responsive field of detectors and actuators, such as water collection/purification systems, micro algae bioreactors and photovoltaic cells that are assimilated in the very 'flesh' of the Homeostatic Membrane.

At the start of the 21st century we are in a unique position with respect to the available technologies to evaluate biological processes with scrutiny never encountered before, and understand them from a bottom-up approach that revolutionises the future potential of architectural design. New visualisation techniques, such as the revolutionary atomic force microscope, allow us to study molecules that exist at a few billionths of a metre. This is the nanoscopic level, which has eluded scrutiny until recently since its scale exists at the wavelengths of visible light and cannot be seen using traditional visualisation techniques.

In 1959 the prophetic Richard Feynman proposed that we could arrange atoms in most of the ways permitted by physical law;[1] and 27 years later K Eric Drexler fleshed out this vision when he published *Engines of Creation: The Coming Era of Nanotechnology*, in which he took inspiration from biological systems to predict the engineering of molecular-scale machines, termed molecular assemblers, that could precisely manipulate and assemble atoms, to create minuscule robots that could carry out industrial-scale functions.[2]

Intriguingly, at the nanoscopic scale, molecules exhibit surprising properties as their unique size influences their behaviour, and materials exhibiting these characteristics are called metamaterials. DaimlerChrysler is working on a new generation of thermoplastics that have been modified by the addition of nanoparticles in a manufacturing process that promises to revolutionise vehicle manufacture and defy traditional Newtonian models of behaviour.[3] Atoms, on the other hand, obey their own physical laws that inhabit the strange world of quantum physics. Uniquely, molecules that lie within the nanometre range possess intermediate properties that are almost impossible to predict. For example, the traditionally inert element gold becomes a catalyst, while changing the size of a particle can alter its colour and electrical resistance unexpectedly.

Nanotechnology can even be employed to improve upon the metamaterials of the natural world to create enhanced, biodegradable woods and foam. Lars Berglund is leading the Biomime project where researchers harvest different types of nanocomposites such as wood and cellulose to improve on their natural properties to make high-performance films, foam and aerogels.[4]

The field of plasmonics is a fascinating area of nanotechnological research where optical signals are transmitted through minuscule structures and can render objects invisible. In 2006, John B Pendry of Imperial College London and his colleagues demonstrated theoretically that a shell of plasmonic metamaterials with unique optical properties could reroute electromagnetic waves travelling through it, thus creating a cloaking device.[5]

It is also possible to combine biological and artificial molecules to create new functional devices at the nano-scale level. Carlo D Montemagno of the University of Cincinnati created an 11-nanometre rotary motor from a bacterial protein and a metallic nanorod that was powered by adenosine triphosphate, the source of chemical energy in cells, and rotated eight times a second.[6] Jim Tour, Chao Professor of Chemistry and director of the Carbon Nanotechnology Laboratory at Rice University's Richard E Smalley Institute for Nanoscale Science and Technology, took the concept of a molecular engine one step further

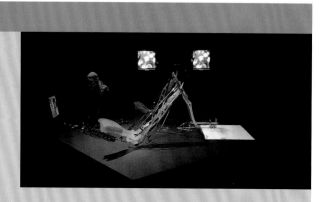

SymbioticA Research Group in collaboration with the Steve Potter Lab, MEART – The Semi Living Artist, 'ArtBots: The Robot Talent Show', Eyebeam Gallery, New York, 2003
The robotic arm is here seen creating drawings on paper. With its 'brain' (dissociated rat neurons grown in culture) growing in Steve Potter's lab in Atlanta, and its body installed at the Eyebeam Gallery in New York, the two interacted through the Internet (TCP/IP) in real time.

A dynamic feedback system was created using a webcam (the eye of MEART) that captured portraits of viewers within the gallery space. These images were then converted into a stimulation map and used to stimulate the neurons (this was the beginning of the drawing process). A multi-channel electrophysiological recording from a neuronal culture (MEART's 'brain') was performed at the Steve Potter Lab, and the resulting data sets were processed in two locations: Atlanta and the Eyebeam Gallery. The processed outcome was used to control and move the drawing arm, and the progress of the drawing was monitored and compared with the original portrait. The difference between the original portrait and the progressing drawing was then sent back to the lab as another stimulation map to complete the feedback loop, the whole process continuing until a threshold of marks on paper was passed which signified the end of a drawing.

The system's neurons were cultured over 64 electrodes fitted on a glass substrate (multi-electrode array – MEA). These electrodes picked up 60 channels of activity from the neurons. The data received from the neural activity was processed both in Atlanta and New York to control the robotic (drawing) arm in real time.

and created a motorised NanoCar that was powered by light,[7] using a modified version of a molecular rotating motor originally designed by Ben L Feringa at the University of Groningen in the Netherlands.[8]

Nanocars and other synthetic transporters may yet prove to be a suitable alternative or additional tool for bottom-up systems where biological methods are not practical to move objects in a controlled fashion on a molecular scale. Nanovehicles could ultimately be incorporated into biological systems to create radically new ways for manipulating biological materials in architectural practice, so that designer organic and inorganic molecules will be able to work together.

Even more radical biocompatible designs have been investigated by Nadrian Seeman at New York University, and others who have shown how the self-assembly properties of DNA can be used to create quite complicated nano-scale structures.[9] DNA has proven to be a particularly versatile molecule, especially since its computing power can be tapped to create tiny machines that can speak directly to living cells. The Seeman Research Group at Austin has created scaffolding on which to assemble designer drugs and DNA machines with moving parts such as nanomechanical sensors, switches and tweezers, which can also be used for more complex robotic functions using techniques that were able to exert precision control of the DNA molecule.

Nanotechnology offers architects the possibility of creating a responsive interface between the interior and exterior of cells creating the infrastructure upon which truly responsive architectural interfaces may be produced. Homeostatic Membrane by Anders Christiansen, a diploma student of Unit 20 at the Bartlett School of Architecture, is a dynamic architecture that draws upon nanoscale engineering and biotechnology, setting the scene for the development of a truly integrated ecological design.

Functional integration with inorganic nanotechnology and the biological world has already been achieved by Charles Lieber, a professor of chemistry at Harvard University, who used a bottom-up approach for the mass fabrication of integrated assemblies between rat cortical neurones and nanowires.[10] The device was capable of bidirectional communication and could control the electrical activity of the cells. The hybrid design is even more interesting than its original biological derivative, since its artificial synapses are the first steps towards building a biocompatible artificial brain.

The SymbioticA Research Group (SARG), an Australian art science collective involving a collaboration between Guy Ben-Ary, Philip Gamblen, Oron Catts and Stuart Bunt, has taken this integration of artificial with biological interfaces a step further. Their project MEART – The Semi Living Artist (MEART, which stands for 'multi-electrode and art', is an entity described by its creators as a 'geographically detached, bio-cybernetic research and development project exploring aspects of creativity and artistry in the age of new biological technologies'), in collaboration with the Steve Potter Lab, is made from living biological matter, mechanics and electronics, and has been given sensors using a motion-capture system and motor system that operates through a robotic arm and is capable of producing observable behaviour in the form of automated drawings.[11]

MEART – The Semi Living Artist, 'Australian Culture Now', Australian Centre for Moving Image (ACMI), Melbourne, Australia, 2004
The Melbourne installation used a control paradigm based on population vector algorithms. This uses information from all areas in the neurons, even those that show a weak response to the stimulus. The robotic arms are drawing, and behind them is a computer screen showing a photo of a man's face, a pixellated black-and-white image, a scrolling text box and some graphs. The only other item on the table is a camera that looks down over the arms at the picture they are drawing. A large screen on the wall behind the table shows a graph, a representation that looks like a glacial landscape.

Position sensors were integrated into the robotic arm for the Melbourne exhibition to further improve the control system. The sensors communicated with the software through a microcontroller system to make the positioning of the arm more accurate than before.

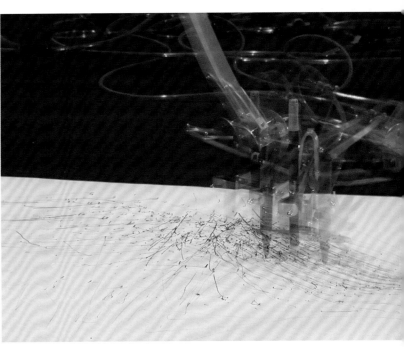

MEART – The Semi Living Artist, 'Biofeel: A New Breed of Artist', Perth Institute of Contemporary Arts, Perth, Australia, 2002
The MEART robotic arm drawing as part of the Biennale for Electronic Arts Perth. In this performance the robot became a geographically detached artist, its 'brain' and 'body' interacting through the Internet (TCP/IP) in real time.

The future implications for architecture in terms of nano-scale modifications to living processes are exciting in that they will form the basis of designer-led, genuinely responsive materials with innovative properties that will have a broad range of applications in our experience of the built environment. ⌂

Notes
1. Richard Feynman's original lecture 'There's Plenty of Room at the Bottom' can be found at www.its.caltech.edu/~feynman/plenty.htm.
2. K Eric Drexler, *Engines of Creation: The Coming Era of Nanotechnology*, Anchor Books (New York), 1986.
3. Daimler Chrysler, 'DaimlerChrysler, suppliers invent recyclable thermoplastic'. See http://findarticles.com/p/articles/mi_hb3381/is_199912/ai_n8122427
4. For more on Lars Berglund's Biomime project, see http://www.biomime.org/archive/june_eng.pdf.
5. For more on John B Pendry's Invisibility Cloak Technology, see http://www.technologynewsdaily.com/node/3076.
6. For more on Carlo D Montemagno's bacterial protein motor and rod, see http://www.springerlink.com/content/x517602072016u67/.
7. For more on Jim Tour's NanoCar, see http://www.21stcentury.co.uk/cars/nano-car.asp.
8. For more on Ben L Feringa's molecular rotating motor, see http://www.nature.com/nature/journal/v440/n7081/full/440163a.html.
9. For more on Nadrian Seeman's flexible DNA experiments, see http://lib.bioinfo.pl/auth:Seeman,NC.
10. For more about the functional integration between inorganic nanotechnology and the biological world, see 'Neuron forms links with silicon nanowires' at http://technology.newscientist.com/article/dn9838.
11. TC&A's *MEART* project can be found at http://www.fishandchips.uwa.edu.au/.

Design for Debate

Advances in biotechnology shift not only the potential skill and knowledge set required of designers, but also, as **Anthony Dunne** explains, the thinking about applications to ethics, as the wider implications of working methods and products have a more far-reaching impact on society. Dunne asked his students at the Royal College of Art in London to respond to this forthcoming challenge by coming up with some pertinent 'what if' scenarios.

Michael Burton, The Race, 2007
Maggot cohabitation device.

As biotech and other advanced technologies move out of the laboratory into the marketplace there is now, more than ever, a need to explore the cultural, social and ethical implications of emerging technologies. Design today is concerned primarily with commercial and marketing activities, but it could operate on a more intellectual level. It could place new technological developments within imaginary but believable everyday situations that would allow us to debate the implications of different technological futures before they happen. This shift from thinking about applications to implications creates a need for new design roles, contexts and methods. It is not only about designing for commercial, market-led contexts, but also for broader societal ones. It is about designing not only products that can be consumed and used today, but also imaginary ones that might exist in years to come. And, it is about imagining not only things we desire, but also undesirable things – cautionary tales that highlight what might happen if we carelessly introduce new technologies into society.

The following design proposals by recent graduates of the MA Design Interactions Course at the Royal College of Art[1] in London explore different ways that thought experiments and 'what if' scenarios can be used, not to predict or anticipate the future, but as tools to help us understand and debate the kind of world we want to live in.

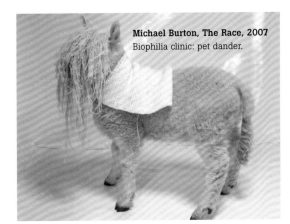

Michael Burton, The Race, 2007
Biophilia clinic: pet dander.

The Race

Michael Burton pushes the edges of speculative design. The Race[2] challenges the current healthcare model of isolating ourselves from natural ecosystems, which is currently in crisis: antibiotics are often no longer effective, and untreatable superbugs like MRSA have begun to emerge. Burton thus sets out an alternative vision for healthcare based on reconnecting ourselves to the ecosystem. It is a purposely provocative position. His project asks us to reconsider ourselves as more than just our DNA, and instead as highly complex, co-evolved organisms: part animal, part conglomeration of bacteria, microbes and parasites. Using short films, photographs and objects he takes us from an alternative present to a distant future.

The first scenario within the project explores the use of maggots to clean up wounds after surgery, which would save huge amounts of money and speed up patient recovery rates. But for most of us, maggots are disgusting and not the sort of thing we would want on, or even in, our bodies despite the benefits.

In Burton's second scenario, he explores biophilia clinics. These are places people could go to increase their exposure to animal dirt and microbes. A favourite is the lamb with extra-long hair which, when it shakes its head, exposes patients to a flurry of bacteria and microbes that we would never normally be exposed to in our over-sanitised and hyper-clean environments, with the intention of making our rather fragile and eroded immune systems more robust. Looking further into the future, he outlines a scenario he calls Future Farm, whereby people volunteer their bodies for 'pharming'; for example where the body might be used to produce chemicals for new medicines.

In the last and most futuristic scenario, people lead an almost fully integrated existence with nature. Fingernails have mutated to pick up more dirt (an exaggeration, but necessary to make the point), and coarse facial hair is used to create cages for crickets and other insects that share our bodies and symbolise this reintegration with nature.

Although set in the near and distant future, these scenarios are by no means predictions or forecasts; their purpose is to spark debate about how our relationship with nature might change in the face of new technological possibilities and the problems with existing approaches to drugs and healthcare.

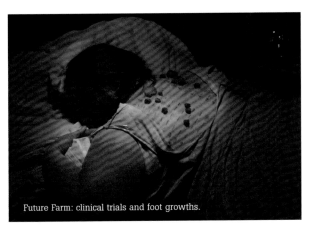

Future Farm: clinical trials and foot growths.

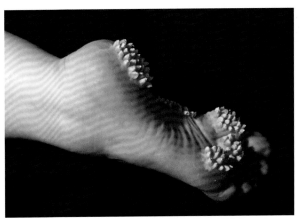

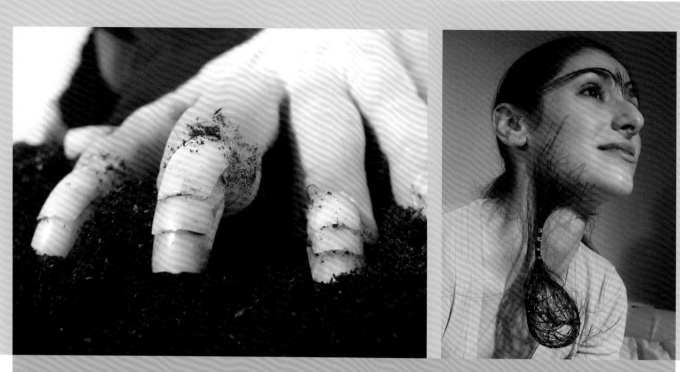

Michael Burton, The Race, 2007
left: Commensal bacteria – fingernails.
right: Hair harbourer.

Marei Wollersberger, Child Force, 2007
far left: Child Force members.
left: Deployment of genetic sensors.

Child Force

Marei Wollersberger's Child Force[3] project is a cautionary tale about the future of childhood presented through a highly aestheticised photo story. It explores the impact of gene technology and its ensuing ideology in relation to our current move towards heightened surveillance. Child Force, a dark version of today's Boy Scouts and Girl Guides, is organised around games and activities for seeking out children with unusual and possibly aberrant behaviour and capturing their DNA for analysis. It invites us to consider questions such as: If scientific findings could be used to decode DNA, will today's children be the first to undergo genetic tests for socially undesirable traits? Would children with 'clean' DNA gain superior status? Could we use genetic engineering to finally make our dream of a safe society reality?

Bee's

All of Susana Soares' projects explore the idea of new organs of perception. Her Bee's[4] project makes reference to the current research into the use of bees to detect explosives. They can be trained in minutes and can also detect hormones and other chemical traces produced by the human body during illness or at different stages of the fertility cycle. Thus one of the more striking proposals to emerge from her project was for an alternative means of diagnosis – less technical and invasive, but also less precise. Bees trained to detect a particular hormone could be placed in a specially designed glass container. The patient would then breathe into a smaller open chamber within the larger one, and if the bees detect the hormone they move into the smaller space, indicating its presence. Like Burton's project above, Bee's is more about opening up a discussion than proposing a real product; in this case, about different ways of living with natural systems and using insects as biosensors.

Susana Soares, Bee's, 2007
New organs of perception.
above: Diagnostic tool.
below: At the beehive.

Although in many cases we cannot yet design actual bioproducts, as the projects described here show we should not let that stop us from getting involved. Speculative designs like these can inspire, raise awareness, stimulate discussion and provoke debate, all of which can help achieve technological futures that reflect the complex, troubled people we are rather than the easily satisfied consumers and users we are supposed to be. Δ

Notes
1. When a first-year project is launched (usually lasting for four weeks), a variety of experts are invited to give talks and help set the agenda. Second-year students are encouraged to develop links with experts during their projects. Invited lecturers included: Professor Richard Jones, nanoscientist; Dr Ian Thompson, bioengineer; Dr Andy Miah, bioethicist; Dr Mark Midownik, materials scientist; Jason Tester, Institute for the Future; Professor Natalie Jeremijenko, artist/designer; and Oron Catts, artist.
2. For The Race project, Burton consulted Peter Openshaw, Professor of Experimental Medicine at Imperial College, London, and Dr Ian Wilson, Senior Principal Scientist at AstraZeneca Plc, as well as the Deptford Creek Environmental Centre, London. His Future Farm scenario was inspired by the work of Richard Jones, Professor of Physics and Senior Strategic Advisor for Nanotechnology for the UK's Engineering and Physical Sciences Research Council, and Dr Oliver Curry, Research Associate, Darwin@LSE (London School of Economics).
3. As part of her research for the project, Wollersberger consulted Horst Voithenleitner, psychologist and director of the International Social Service (ISS) in Vienna, about our current understanding of the social role of children and how optimisation of our genetic make-up could impact on this.
4. Soares' project was supported by David Perkins of the London Beekeeper Association; Dr Glen Rains, College of Agricultural and Environmental Sciences, University of Georgia, US; and Dr Tim Haarmann from the Los Alamos Stealthy Insect Sensor Project, New Mexico.

Ethics, Architecture and Little Soft Machinery

Through his drawings and narrative, **Neil Spiller** evokes a cybernetic world of reflexive spaces and symbolism. Here he explains how the breaking down of the boundaries between landscape and architecture, and a focus on biotechnology and ethics, allows him to straddle the real and the possible.

Neil Spiller, Genetic Gazebo, 2005
The internal apparatus of the Genetic Gazebo showing the 16-point electrode array and the amber.

Catching Nature's Breath in the Genetic Gazebo

It was midsummer and the rain was fresh on the ground. The smell of nature's verdant newborn organic jewels was in the air and occasionally the nasty niff of farm effluent wafted across the boy's sore and streaming nostrils. He squared up to the old gazebo; the millpond and its little weir were on his right and rattling in his ears. All was as it should be except for the metallic armature, one end dipped into the agitated water, the other end disappearing through the window of the gazebo. The boy scrabbled up the wall using eroded arrises as footholds, his little chest heaving with the exertion. He focused his eyes through the unglazed window. All was dark inside, but as his eyes grew accustomed to the light the first thing he noticed was the soft glow of amber light. A musty smell greeted his nose. This place had the smell of a greenhouse or a church. He just knew that strange things happened here. He also knew that that smell would bring on an asthma attack, as nature's terrible spores agitated his pink little tubes. Despite the ongoing tightening in his chest, he edged closer. The silhouettes of two Doric columns stood across the room framed by the outside light, looking like obscene guardians from another era protecting an architecture that had long since mutated into a series of electric pulses, potential differences and fur machines that probed the particularity of all things and fed on itself. Between the columns in the bright air outside, a birdbath, the silky shine of a freshly watered feather creating a pleasing quick glint of light. Why was that mouse in the corner not moving?

He had had enough; he dropped to the ground, silently against the interference of the weir. He grasped for his inhaler in his coat, dusted the brick dust and water off his raincoat and enjoyed instant bronchial relief. He noticed the new scratch on the cheap plastic buckle of the raincoat. He would return later, perhaps when they said its ceiling was woven, and when the conkers were out … enough now! Another buckle on his leather sandal was chafing. He limped off …

Communicating Vessels

This small essay concerns itself with a subset of architectonic spaces and ideas that are included in my 10-year research project Communicating Vessels, and specifically the Genetic Gazebo and Little Soft Machinery. These proposals form part of a cybernetic system of reflexive inputs, outputs and symbolism. The status of the outputs and inputs are always in flux and often choreographed by chance. This text illustrates how it is possible, while utilising advanced technologies, to create a cybernetic universe of discourse that blooms in a variety of interesting, intellectual and interstitially unstable ways. It is within this personal epistemology of art and architecture that the old dichotomies between landscape and building disappear and issues of biotechnology and ethics become relevant.

Like Alfred Jarry's *Doctor Faustroll*,[1] a doctor of pataphysics, we will journey to strange places. We will meet strange people, glands, genes, pets and unborn artists, all of which will serve to remind us that we inhabit augmented and mixed space of our own and others' making. If nature's imperatives and vectors can be sensed and used as drivers for architecture, then the possibilities of reflexively embroidering the architectural become infinite. Humanity's ability to perceive the full gamut of architectural space within the electromagnetic spectrum is limited without technological augmentation.

The Communicating Vessels project is situated on an island in Fordwich, Kent (near where I grew up). It is a 10-year research project that seeks to illustrate the far-reaching effects on architecture of biotechnology, virtuality and nanotechnology, and particularly the old division between landscape and architecture. The project relooks at traditional paradigms such as the gazebo, the shed, the dovecote and the bower, and explores a reflexive series of relationships between them. It also includes a robotic Baroness who lives in a Bower and some riverside seats called 'Dee Stools'.

Harvester of Eyes

Now is an exciting time to be an architect. Technology is allowing architects to mix and augment the actual with the virtual, to question the inertness of materials and, vicariously, architecture, to link and network all manner of spaces and phenomena, create reflexive spatial

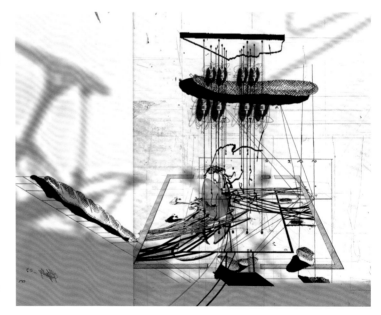

Neil Spiller, Genetic Gazebo, 2005
A composite drawing of the Genetic Gazebo and its context within the Communicating Vessels project.

relationships, blend the organic and the inorganic and be non-Luddite about ecology and sustainability. Simultaneously, the aged doctrines of Modernism are being questioned; decoration and baroque distortion are respectable again. The 'everyday' has proved a fecund breeding ground for new ideas. Manufacturing processes are being liberated from manual calculation and time-consuming fabrication protocols; digital craft is having its genesis. Collaborative working practices are dissolving previously jealously defended distinct disciplinary boundaries. Narrative is also finding its way into architectural work. Above all, architecture's new relationship with biotechnology is evolving, and evolving fast.

One of the first touchstones for me when considering architecture and biotechnology is an illustration done hundreds of years ago by Hieronymous Bosch. It features a tree inhabited by an owl (a Boschian symbol for the Devil); in the copse behind the tree are ears, and strewn in the foreground are eyes. Through contemporary eyes I view this picture as a thought experiment in the husbanding of flesh and its inherent ethical and evil implications.

Dendritic Genetics

The Genetic Gazebo is inspired by the cybernetician Gordon Pask and his development of a self-wiring, 'evolving' electric circuit. Pask's electrochemical assemblage consisted of an electrode array immersed in a liquid ferrous sulphate medium. Fluctuating dendritic circuitry was formed by electrical charges precipitating conducting material from the ferrous sulphate solution. As the position of the charges changed or remained (conditioned by outside stimuli), the circuitry changed or further strengthened itself. I have used such a cybernetic self-wiring system to generate geometries and dimensions that are used as input data for another machine in the Communicating Vessels project (which is not described in this article). As the external input stimuli for the Genetic Gazebo I used three different systems, two of which were genetic inputs. The array I used was a 4 x 4, 16-point electrical array, whereby charges can be formed between any of the 16 points. Whichever points are electrified, and when, is conditioned by the switching between three sources of data: a quadripartite birdbath, a prehistoric insect's DNA encased in amber, and the DNA of an old childhood pet of mine who died in 1976 – a gerbil called Micky. All of these drivers are four-variable codes, including the birdbath, which selects each of its coordinates depending on which of its four quarters is being used at the time. Therefore combinations of genetic data and the movements of birds can be transformed into points and relationships that can be then used as geometries to make other things. Polemically, therefore,

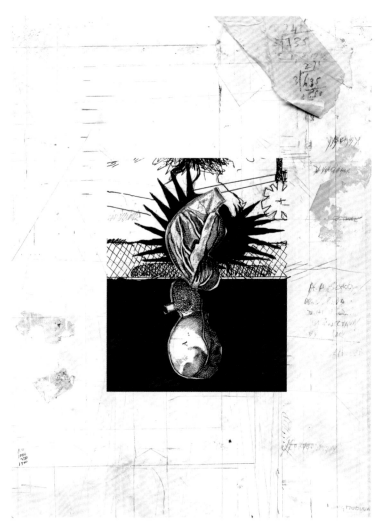

Neil Spiller, Little Soft Machinery, 2006
Detail of bladder, almost empty: no cars recently.

this architectural piece enquires into issues of genetics, memory, and the use of the dead as drivers for new architectures. Such preoccupations are further explored in the second piece that I wish to describe from the Communicating Vessels project.

The Story of Little Soft Machinery

The boy was out late, but even so he stopped outside the Angel Gate. A car went past; there was a rustling in the underground. Suddenly, what seemed out of nowhere the professor strode up to him, the clip of cowboy boots clacking on the rainbowed tarmac. The professor crouched down suppressing a Fremlins belch. The boy smelt the hops on his breath as he whispered into the boy's ear: 'Defy the logic of alphabets, run with thy swerve, embrace the spiral, I am clinaman, I am chinaman.' Slightly frightened the boy recoiled and the professor tapped the side of his nose; simultaneously the smell of gasoline and a just audible groan issued from ground level. The boy jumped on his bicycle and was off to another time. It is said that the professor has a garden of what on Earthly Delights.

'You are a brave boy to lean your bicycle up against Lillith's gate Sonny,' the professor shouted after him.

Somewhere there is a Little Soft Machinery, a magic creature like you or me but not like you or me. It grew up out of some stem cells, an old testicle and a leaky bladder. He does things by desire. And Little Soft Machinery lives on the island and under the foot of Truth, below the bush pressed between angels' wings. On the island there are a lot of systems he plays with like the Dee Stools and the Baroness. He makes grease for them and they love him. The Professor watches him work and the weight of the foot makes him not contain himself.

Little Soft Machinery is a seed box and a little Erector Set, self-repairing, he thinks of delightful things.

In 1926 a little-remembered children's book was published in America. An extraordinary story illustrated by the author's Picarbia-esque drawings, *Little Machinery* was written and illustrated by Mary Liddell, and Nathalie op de Beeck describes it thus:

This book signals the uneasy encounter between competing concepts of childhood: that of a Golden Age youth allied with nature versus the 'modern' child, who tinkers with miniature machines, understands his or her identity in relation to mechanical objects, and conceives of a future as an engineer or builder. *Little Machinery* provides a singular, and now almost forgotten, fairy tale of modernity. The Little Machinery, a mechanical boy, is 'a magic creature'. Unlike the fairies and elves that captivated the British Victorians and their middle-class admirers and successors abroad, he is composed of spare parts from obsolete manmade devices. 'He grew up out of some pieces of a steam engine that was in a wreck, an old trolley car that couldn't run any more, and a broken automobile,' and so appears to have generated himself from objects that no longer work. He might be described as a self-propelled, fictive realization of the fanciful belief in haunted machinery, the ghost in and of the machine. If so, he is an unforeseen, artificial, and not entirely welcome entity arising from an overabundance of broken-down material goods, in a fast-paced industrial culture more interested in replacing than repairing used objects. His existence presupposes the presence of junkyards, where worn-out engines are divested of their useful metal parts and then tossed in a trash heap. His strange revitalization, independent of human assistance, carries a vague threat. *Little Machinery* places a metaphysical, synchronic dimension in uneasy contact with diachronic change and a rational universe.[2]

Neil Spiller, Angel Gate, 2006
Angel Gate is the entrance portal to the Communicating Vessels island. Little Soft Machinery nestles on the ground in the centre below the bush pressed between angels' wings.

Little Soft Machinery is my 21st-century reworking of this older model, recast as a biomechanical desiring fleshed object. Little Soft Machinery is not very smart, just smart enough to desire, which provokes his biomechanical glands to produce the grease, the vaz or the holy gasoline (this substance is called many things: it changes lives, it mixes chance). It is a nanotech elixir, smart but highly explosive (the Communicating Vessels project is in part powered by the grease and the holy gasoline). The Baroness calls it holy gasoline and blows it into fiery bubbles out of one of her face tubes, letting off steam as her cast-iron lover teeters away, distant yet intimately connected.

Little Soft Machinery lusts after cars; he is a contemporary Marinetti. As every car passes him by, he revels in its pungent exhaust, fast vibrations and shapes. These inputs excite his secreting mechanism and a drop of holy gasoline is produced. Eventually his bladder becomes so full that it cannot resist the weight of the foot of Truth, and it expels its contents all over the road, from where the grease wanders off to the Baroness or to the Alembics (another part of the Communicating Vessels project).

In conclusion there is little here that is impossible: fluorescent rabbits have been bred, and stem cells have been wired up to drawing machines (what status has art when its artist was never born?). Australian performance artist Stelarc has grown an ear on his arm and many, many more polemic biotechnical art projects have been created. It is now time for architects to address these very important issues.

Now shall I make a waistcoat for Little Soft Machinery or not? I kind of care about him you see: as I made him, he is my responsibility. ∆

Note
1. Alfred Jarry, *Exploits and Opinions of Doctor Faustroll, Pataphysician* in *Alfred Jarry, Three Early Novels – Collected Works II*, Atlas Press (London), 2006. Originally published in French in 1911.
2. Nathalie op de Beeck, '"The First Picture Book for Modern Children": Mary Liddell's *Little Machinery* and the Fairy Tale of Modernity', *Children's Literature* 32, Hollins University (Roanoke, VI), 2004.

Contributors

Sean Affleck is a director of Make Architects, a studio of highly creative and imaginative architects and designers committed to designing buildings, spaces and places that are as striking and innovative as they are socially, economically and environmentally responsible. The practice was founded by Ken Shuttleworth in 2004 and has already established itself as one of the UK's foremost architectural firms, with over 130 employees based in studios in London, Edinburgh and Birmingham. Make's first award-winning building was completed in 2006 and the practice currently has more than 300 projects under way, ranging in scale from residential towers, office developments, mixed-use schemes and urban masterplans to civic buildings, interior design and low-cost housing projects.

Rachel Armstrong is a writer, television presenter, multimedia producer and general medical practitioner specialising in non-Darwinian techniques of evolution and challenges of the extraterrestrial environment. She is the author and producer of a large number of multimedia projects ranging from printed literature to virtual reality and Internet programs. Her first science-fiction novel *The Gray's Anatomy* was published in 2001 by Serpent's Tail. She was also editor of an *Art & Design* issue entitled 'Sci-fi Aesthetics', released in 1997 by Wiley-Academy, and 'Space Architecture' for *AD* in 2001. She has published extensively on post-human evolution and alien phenomena, working at the intersection of art, science and technology.

The Tissue Culture and Art Project (TC&A) initiated by **Oron Catts** and **Ionat Zurr** in 1996 is an ongoing research and development project into the use of tissue technologies as a medium for artistic expression. TC&A was a model for, and is now based in SymbioticA – The Centre of Excellence in Biological Arts, School of Anatomy and Human Biology, the University of Western Australia. Oron Catts, a co-founder and director of SymbioticA, is an artist/researcher and a curator. Originally trained in product design and after having gained a BA focusing on the future interaction of design and biological derived technologies, he went on to gain an MA in visual art. Ionat Zurr is an artist/researcher and an academic coordinator of SymbioticA. Both have exhibited and published internationally. They have recently exhibited as part of the 'sk-interface' exhibition in Liverpool and the 'Design and Elastic Mind' exhibition at the Museum of Modern Art (MoMA), New York.

Peter Cook is Professor of Architecture at the Royal Academy of Arts in London and Emeritus Professor of both University College London (UCL) and the Städelschule in Frankfurt, Germany. He was the founder of Archigram, the apocryphal British group who were awarded the Royal Gold Medal for Architecture in 2003. He is the architect (with Colin Fournier) of the Kunsthaus Graz in Austria, and of apartment buildings in Berlin and Madrid. His own drawings are in the collections of the Museum of Modern Art (MoMA) in New York, the Centre Pompidou in Paris, the Deutsches Architekturmuseum in Frankfurt, FRAC in Orléans, France, the V&A in London and the Japan Architect Collection in Tokyo, as well as many private collections. In 2007, he received a knighthood for services to education and architecture, and with his office Crab Studio Architects he is about to build a municipal theatre for Verbania in Italy.

Marcos Cruz is a lecturer and tutor of Unit 20 at the Bartlett School of Architecture, UCL, and a visiting lecturer and tutor of DS10 at the University of Westminster. He is also a co-director of marcosandmarjan, a London-based office that combines practice and teaching of architecture with experimental design research. He gained his diploma from the ESAP Porto, and a masters and PhD degree from the Bartlett. His research and office work has been published and exhibited widely, including at the São Paulo Biennial in 2003, the Venice Biennale in 2004 and the iCP 2005. In 2000 he was part of the design team for the Kunsthaus Graz competition with Peter Cook and Colin Fournier (first prize). He is co-editor of the publication *Unit 20* (University of Valencia/ACTAR, 2002) and co-author of *Interfaces/Intrafaces*, a monographic documentation of the work of marcosandmarjan (iCP/SpringerWienNewYork, 2005).

Anthony Dunne is Professor and Head of the Design Interactions Department at the Royal College of Art in London, and a partner in the design practice Dunne & Raby. He is the author of *Hertzian Tales: Electronic Products, Aesthetic Experience, and Critical Design* (MIT Press, 2006) and co-author of *Design Noir: The Secret Life of Electronic Objects* (Birkhauser, 2001). His work has been exhibited at the Museum of Modern Art (MoMA) in New York, the Centre Pompidou, Paris, and the Science Museum in London.

Nicola Haines studied architecture at the Bartlett School of Architecture, UCL, between 1992 and 1999. She has worked with HB Design in Hong Kong, and Foster + Partners and Allies and Morrison in London. In 2004 she co-founded Tierney Haines Architects (www.tierneyhaines.com) with her husband Stephen Tierney in Dublin where they live.

Tobias Klein studied architecture at the RWTH Aachen, the University of Applied Arts in Vienna (masterclass of Wolf Prix) and finished his studies at the Bartlett School of Architecture, UCL (Distinction in Design, Commendation RIBA Silver Medal 2006; Winner ARCH+ prize 2006; Royal Academy summer show exhibitor and winner of the student prize 2006). He worked for Coop Himmelb(l)au in Vienna and is currently working as a 3-D design consultant for several London-based offices including Andrew Wright Associates (Young Architect of the Year 2000). He taught at the University of Greenwich and the London South Bank University, as well as on a consultant basis for the University of Syracuse, New York. He is currently teaching at the Royal College of Art as a tutor of Design Studio 1 (ADS1) and is a founding member of HoRhizon, a research design platform.

Sulan Kolatan is the co-founder, with William MacDonald, of Kol/Mac LLC. She received her MS in Architecture and Building Design from Columbia University and holds a Dipl Ing Arch from the RWTH Aachen, Germany. She taught at the GSAP at Columbia University from 1999 to 2005, and served as Acting Chair of the Department of Architectural Design and Building Technology at the Technical University in Darmstadt from 2002 to 2003. William MacDonald is Chair of the Graduate Architecture and Design Program at Pratt Institute in New York. He holds an MS in Architecture and Urban Design from Columbia University and a BArch from Syracuse University. He attended the Architectural Association in London and Cornell University Sommer Akademie in Berlin. He taught at the Graduate School of Architecture, Planning, and Preservation at Columbia from 1985 to 2005, during which time he directed various graduate programmes. They have each served as visiting chair and critic at a number of distinguished universities, and frequently lecture at academic and professional conferences internationally. Their collaborative practice has received numerous honours and awards.

Steve Pike spent a number of years as a designer before he studied at the Bartlett School of Architecture, UCL, receiving a masters degree in 2003. He continues to pursue his research, founding arColony (www.arcolony.com), a forum for experimental architecture. His work has been included in a number of publications and international exhibitions. He is currently practising with Acanthus LW Architects in London.

François Roche is a co-founder, with Stéphanie Lavaux and Jean Navarro, of R&Sie(n), a Paris-based office that was set up in 1989. The organic, oppositional architectural projects of their practice are concerned with the bond between building, context and human relations. Roche explains his concept of 'spoiled climate' architecture as a means to create protocols in apparatuses that merge fiction, subjectivation and processes of transformation with 'bachelors and desirable' machines, simultaneously re-scenariosing the aesthetic relationship with nature(s): artificial, paranoiac and/or real. The firm's projects have been exhibited at Tate Modern (2006), Columbia University (1999–2000), UCLA (1999–2000), the ICA (London, 2001), Mori Art Museum Tokyo (2004), Centre Pompidou (2004), MAM Paris (2005, 2006), the MIT Media Lab (2006), and Orléans/ArchiLab (1999, 2001, 2003). Their work will be part of the next Venice Biennale in the International Italian pavilion.

Neil Spiller is Professor of Architecture and Digital Theory, Graduate Architecture Programmes Director, Director of the Advanced Virtual and Technological Architecture Research Group (AVATAR) and Vice Dean at the Bartlett School of Architecture, UCL. He is author of many books on architecture and cyberspace including *Digital Dreams: Architecture and the New Alchemic Technologies* (Watson-Guptill Publications, 1998), *Cyberreader: Critical Writings for the Digital Era* (Phaidon, 2002) and *Visionary Architecture: Blueprints of the Modern Imagination* (Thames & Hudson, 2006). He has also guest-edited several issues of *AD*. In 2002 he was John and Magda McHale Research Fellow at the State University of New York at Buffalo. His book *Digital Architecture NOW*, a compendium of contemporary digital architectural practice, will be published by Thames & Hudson during autumn 2008.

Yukihiko Sugawara is a practising architect. He studied as part of the Yamashita Studio at the Nagaoka Institute of Design, Japan, and at the Bartlett School of Architecture, UCL, where he received a masters degree in 2004. His academic work has been published internationally.

Ton Venhoeven is architect/director of VenhoevenCS Architects (www.venhoevencs.nl), Professor of Architectural History and Theory at the Technical University of Eindhoven, and adviser to the national government on infrastructure. He established VenhoevenCS Architects in Amsterdam in 1998. The creative team forms an innovative office for sustainable architecture, urban planning and infrastructure. The office's research focuses on the design of self-supporting cities and emissions-free buildings. The social and cultural aspects are of great importance in the firm's projects, the CS in its name making reference to this. VenhoevenCS produces a variety of public and private works, ranging from housing projects, interior design and utilitarian buildings to infrastructure, urban design and development research. It has been recognised with numerous publications, awards and exhibitions in the Netherlands and abroad. A monograph on the practice is due for publication in 2008.

Bill Watts is a senior partner at Max Fordham LLP. Following a university education in biological science, he has spent 26 years developing the firm's reputation for designing elegant buildings with a thorough understanding of how they are put together, how the environment affects comfort, and in particular how energy can be used and minimised to make buildings comfortable. He has worked with leading designers on a broad range of projects, and more recently has conducted wider studies into how the UK could be self-sufficient for its energy needs from local renewable energy resources, linking this to a study of the use of land to produce food and energy, and the use of waste as a resource. This research was presented at the 2006 World Renewable Energy Conference (WREC) in Florence. He has worked with the Carbon Trust in Northern Ireland, investigating methods of utilising waste to produce energy and other resources, and is currently working with architects and academics to explore the cooling benefits of green walls to rid cities of the urban heat island effect, with a number of installations planned for the UK over the coming year.

AD+ CONTENTS

World Expo 2008 Zaragoza

This summer, Expo 2008 at Zaragoza, in Aragon in Spain, splashed on to the planet with the theme of 'Water and Sustainable Development'. Though the subject of the exposition was driven by the recent controversies surrounding Spain and Aragon's management of water, **Mark Garcia** outlines how the Expo investigated these issues in a way that was relevant to the rest of the world, delivering in just three months an impressive contribution to national and international debates about the problems and future of water.

Bridge Pavilion (Zaha Hadid Architects)
View from the north bank towards the south, from the eastern underside of the bridge.

Aerial-view computer rendering of Expo site. Top left is the newly constructed 3rd Millennium Bridge by Arenas & Partners, and below is Zaha Hadid's Bridge Pavilion. To the right is the white, jagged, six-storey Conference Centre by Fuensanta Nieto and Enrique Sobejano (Nieto Sobejano arquitectos), and Enrique De Teresa's Water Tower. Olano y Mendos arquitectos' Aragon Pavilion can be seen bottom right.

Though most Expo 'cities' vanish, many go on to become successful urban parks. Zaragoza, however, has gone a step further than this and has dealt with its critics and rivals by promoting the Expo as a regenerative engine for the city.

A new cable car takes visitors over the river to the Expo site from Ricardo Bofill's Zaragoza-Delicias Intermodal Station (1999), Spain's largest transport interchange. The Expo site sits on the Ranillas meander of the voluminous River Ebro, and with over 140 pavilions that represented 102 countries is spread over a total of 25 hectares (61.7 acres). Its four main axes are casually bordered on two sides by a continuous, roughly L-shaped, two-storey block of undulating, brightly striped city-wall-type, blobby Pop-urbanism. These two building strips break down into four or five similar appendix buildings which move down the slope towards the river bank and during the Expo, which ran from 14 June to 14 September, housed the main Spanish and regional pavilions

Between this connective urban tissue are the six permanent architectural elements that remain on the site now that the circus has left town: Olano y Mendos arquitectos' Aragon Pavilion; Fuensanta Nieto and Enrique Sobejano's (Nieto Sobejano arquitectos) Conference Centre; Enrique De Teresa's Water Tower; Zaha Hadid's Bridge Pavilion; Patxi Mangado's Spanish Pavilion; and Alvaro Planchuelo's Aquarium. There were also seven smaller, temporary pavilions and thematic plazas, all surrounded by a 120-hectare (296.5-acre) landscaped water park designed by Iñaki Alday, Margarita Jover and Cristine Dalnoky.

Aragon Pavilion (Olano y Mendos arquitectos)
top: Derived from the forms of traditional, woven Aragonese basketwork, the pavilion building is supported on three fat, supporting pillars. The plans show a dispersed set of geometrically faceted and coloured cores that pierce and rise up, distorting through the floor plates before they break through the roof to become smaller roof-top pavilions.

Conference Centre (Fuensanta Nieto and Enrique Sobejano/Nieto Sobejano arquitectos)
centre: The deeply folded elevation and cartoon mountain-range skyline of this six-storey, flexible, multi-programme event building define one side of the Expo's largest open public space.

Digital Water Pavilion (Carlo Ratti Associati)
bottom: A fountain building, this habitable pavilion's water-sheet walls worked like a giant inkjet printer. The streams of high-frequency, programmable jets of water were controlled by minutely spaced rows of solenoid valves.

Water Tower (Enrique De Teresa)
At 76 metres (249 feet) tall, the Water Tower is the Expo site's dominant vertical element. Its central atrium contained the *Splash* sculpture by Programme Collective.

Splash **(Programme Collective)**
One of the largest and most audacious sculptural examples of complex, freeform, digital design, manufacturing and construction in the world, this splash of water in motion, caught in time and suspended in mid-air, was one of the Expo's most memorable and striking highlights.

Located on the opposite bank of the Ebro, just before the north entrance to Hadid's bridge, was the Digital Water Pavilion by Carlo Ratti Associati of the MIT SENSEable City Laboratory. This is a high-tech reworking of Mies' Barcelona Pavilion (1928–9). A single-storey rectangle in plan, its wraparound walls consisted of a digitally controlled curtain of falling water. Dropping through thin metal grilles straight through the floor, the curtain magically 'opened' to allow visitors to walk through the wall of water. The computer-controlled and interactive nature of these water screens meant that they fell with gaps of air and water, appearing to 'move' sideways and diagonally, generating a continuously scrolling pattern of pixels. Sadly, however, the resolution did not allow for clear typography or images, though it did create some poetic, moving patterns and sound effects. Covered in a thin sheet of water, the roof was also supported on piston-columns that could move up and down the height of the building; thus, when the roof was down and the water walls switched off, the envelope and therefore most of the building evaporated.

Enrique De Teresa's Water Tower, a corporate, developer's style glass-covered structure, is situated to the north of the Conference Centre. It consists, on plan, of 23 uncompromisingly identical floor plates all in the form of a drop of water. However, the big surprise comes when, on ascending an escalator from the ground floor to the first floor, one realises there are no further floor plates: the rest of the tower is almost entirely hollow except for a gigantic 20-storey frozen 'splash' of (what looks like) mercury, suspended in mid-air, at the centre of the tower's void. This stunning *pièce de résistance* is by far the most artful and futuristic sculpture on the Expo site. As one walks up the ascending, two-person-wide ramp that spirals around the 'splash' (and which is the only 'floor' space inside this atrium), it becomes apparent that the building is the attenuated, etiolated twin to Frank Lloyd Wright's Guggenheim Museum in New York (1959). The generosity/waste of space in this building makes it seem like architectural packaging, and it will be a challenge to the curators of the museum/cultural centre it is destined to become post-Expo.

However, it was Zaha Hadid's Bridge Pavilion – Zaragoza's answer to Bilbao's Guggenheim – that stole the show. One of the few pedestrian building-bridges in the world, it instantly became an iconic masterpiece. Flowing over the River Ebro in a sleek 260-metre (853-foot) span, its 7,000 tonnes of steel and concrete vary in height between 15 and 30 metres (49.2 and 98.4 feet), and between 8 and 30 metres (26.2 and 98.4 feet) in width. The structure is made up of two interlocking surfaces. The first is a single, apparently monocoque underside in dark grey that touches both banks of the river and swoops down to and up from the river on a streamlined conical foot. This deck supports the second, more complex set of surfaces and structures above, which consist of a series of triangular sections, set 3.6 metres (11.8 feet) apart, covered with a steel diagrid structural net. Set to the triangular sections on the bias, this creates a sheath that covers the bridge and forms a kind of elongated pod. At one node, the pod trifurcates into three similar pods that launch themselves, on ballistic, refracting trajectories, at the opposite bank. These vectors are expressed and exert themselves vertically, forming a muscular and

Bridge Pavilion (Zaha Hadid Architects)
Aerial view of the west elevation of the bridge, from the top of the Water Tower.

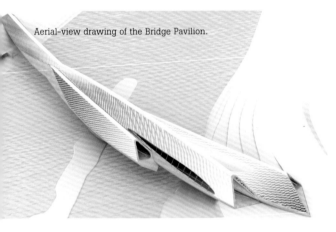

Aerial-view drawing of the Bridge Pavilion.

cinematic series of variable waves and ripples which, like force fields, push and pull splits into the skin, creating the effect of continuous and gymnastic variations in the interiors of the hollow sections of the pods. This generates an external and internal dialectic between the dynamic of the forms evolving with and against each other to give a sense of a precise piloting of the forms in motion. Such controlled attention to the overall movement and navigation of the forms of the interiors and the exterior, as well as the detailing, gives the space a kinetic equipoise that bears the mark of advanced parametric design.

The bridge exterior has traces of hard, engineering-driven, high-performance and high-speed military and armoured articulations. But there is also a softer, more organic zoomorphic and natural sensibility to its forms. Fish, reptiles, rays, gladioli, sharks and other more viscous, energetic forms seem to be reflected in the overall design and in the detailing of the razzle-dazzle, Op Art patterning on the sinusoidal external elevations. The sophisticated moiré-effect skin of seemingly aperiodic

tiling is particularly striking. This is not just because it is so complex and works so well to enhance the dynamics of the forms, but also because it plays hypnotic, pulsating tricks on the eye, the triangular monochromatic patterns making it hard to fixate on or to comprehend the true form, direction and depth of surface. In the right light conditions, for example when strong sunlight is reflected by and bounces off the river, or under the light of a full moon, the disruptive gradients of the bridge's reticulated surfaces begin to dematerialise and liquefy the structure's pods. On an overcast day and at night, it is more like a kaleidoscopic series of parked, overlapping high-speed trains.

From both north and south river banks, one is introduced, at the entrance/windows, to the literally overarching formal concept of the parabolic triangular section. The triangle is the most efficient geometric form for the computer to manipulate and efficiently manufacture, and is also used for the triangular shingles used to make the skin shimmer. The pod forms protect the bridge from the strong Aragonese sunlight and the Tramontana wind that blows down the Ebro. Reminiscent of the inclined, curved entrance to Melnikov's proposal for a Garage Bridge in Paris (1925), the large-scale use of the triangular section to create an inner-habitable structure also has a precedent in Team Luscher's unbuilt design for a bridge across Lake Geneva (1994). While the lower supporting substructure might recall the one-foot-in-the-river styling of Branson Coates' Bridge City (1996) and the flattened, filleted, ellipsoid windows and streamlining of Future Systems' People's Bridge project (1996), the true precedents are Hadid's own bridges, particularly her exploded, competition-winning habitable bridge across the Thames in London (1996).

Influenced by shipbuilding methods, the bridge structure solves the problems of how to support and join four 'pods' based on a series of changing diamond-shaped, stacked and interlocking, double-decked sections. Each pod, apart from the smallest, has an upper deck, and as can be seen from the section drawings, at various points the structural systems and nodal points of the pods are used to brace and stabilise

each other and to suspend and support the various interlacings of the ramps and decks that form the circulation system. The structural systems here are exploited to provide carefully choreographed views, both internally and externally.

From both banks, one feels both propelled out of and sucked into the bridge by the sloping tunnel entrances, over which are suspended the white, prow-like tongue decks of the upper floors. These are suggestive of Melnikov, and are a reminder that Hadid's 1976 final-year project at the Architectural Association in London was 'Malevich's Tektonik', which included a 14-level bridge across the Thames. Once inside the Zaragoza Bridge Pavilion, one is moved around on a series of imperceptible travelators, by a kind of architectural peristalsis. The snaking, double-backing, multiple-choice routes and the more visceral, skeletal and cartilaginous interiors are perfect for meandering *paseos*, and deconstruct the normal linear trajectories of most other bridges.

Some of the external shingles are on hinges and allow a constantly varying kinetic pattern of sunlight to play across the interiors, projecting go-faster arrows around the structure. At night they activate and further complicate, lighten and diffuse the pod's patterns. Considering that this bridge is based on Hadid's two previous designs for bridges over the Thames, the English should be crying with jealousy and humiliation for not yet having a Hadid bridge in London.

View of the west elevation from the north bank, looking south. The Ebro is prone to flooding, thus the ends of Hadid's bridge touch ground high up on the banks of the river.

View of the interior of the bridge from the south entrance towards the north bank. Parts of the Conference Centre and the Water Tower can be seen through the west-facing window.

An unexpectedly organic, biomorphic and sensuous view from the south bank of the conical foot and springing point of the quadrafurcating central node.

The Future for Expos

The Zaragoza Expo did not completely shy away from presenting some of the ugly, difficult problems of natural and man-made water disasters, including global thirst and environmental crises, or the effects of political, corporate, social and economic mismanagement of water. It tackled the various multidisciplinary aspects of water well, and convincingly presented a thorough, well-designed treatment of the problems as well as attempting to bring the world together to find solutions. Expos are also about events and conferences, and the Zaragoza offering succeeded in bringing together more than 2,000 academics, professionals and researchers to produce a 'Zaragoza Charter' to try to solve some of the world's pressing water problems.

Criticism of the Expo, however, has come from closer to home.[1] The other two provinces of the Aragon region, Huesca and Teruel, have complained of disinvestment in their infrastructures, and of negative environmental impacts from Zaragoza's water-management activities. Aragon and Zaragoza also have their own quarrels with the Spanish central government's ideas about diverting scarce water from the Ebro to other parts of Spain.

Expos are seemingly value for money for participating countries, according to an economic study of the 2000 Hanover Expo by Tjaco Walvis.[2] While the Zaragoza Expo soaked up around €700 million of investment (€2,500 million was invested in the city as a whole), at the time of writing the authorities are refusing to release details as to the costs of specific buildings and projects, making it impossible to make a final judgement on the value and significance of these. This said, the long-term urban, cultural and economic benefits of the Expo seem secure: its legacy has been strategically well planned (the site is becoming a cultural, leisure and business park) and the London Olympics should take note.

The idea of a themed Expo and its longer-term legacy seems to have worked so well in Zaragoza that one imagines every subsequent Expo will address similar types of issues. However, it is unlikely that themes such as war, terrorism, nuclear weapons, drugs, poverty, starvation, crime, disease, racism, death, feminism, disablement, homosexuality, Tibet, Burma, Palestine, religion, capitalism or their antitheses will be popular. It is certainly unlikely that you will find any of these issues addressed in any pavilions at the next Expo in Shanghai in 2010. Would they be addressed in a London Expo (there has not been one since 1868)?

Just as one day the international community should give an Expo to South America and Africa (these continents have never hosted one, and Asia only joined the Expo club in 1968), perhaps one day the world might also begin to address these problems in the same way that Zaragoza has addressed water. Until they do, Expos will never do enough.

The Zaragoza Expo will hopefully lead the way for future Expos in proposing that it is not enough just to reflect on the present or to design useless, pleasurable, otherworldly and entertaining spectacles; design must help to galvanise international action on a specific problem or topic. Thus the design and visualisation of useful, radical and critical future Expos could help us choose alternative futures for ourselves, and encourage us to make action, change and innovation a reality. Δ+

Mark Garcia is the Research Co-ordinator of the Department of Architecture at the Royal College of Art in London, and was guest-editor of the *Architextiles* issue of *AD* (Nov/Dec 2006). His forthcoming publications include *The Diagrams of Architecture*, to be published by John Wiley & Sons Ltd in 2009, and the *AD* issue *Patterns of Architecture* (Nov/Dec 2009).

Acknowledgements
Thanks to Jeronimo Blasco (Expo Director of Operations), Ricardo Martin Tezanos (Expo Director of Press), Manuela Gatto (Zaha Hadid Architects) and Anna Jackson (V&A Museum) for interviews, to Pilar Balet (Expo Press) for her guided tours of the Expo, to Tom Barker and Nigel Coates (Royal College of Art) for funding and support for my Expo research, and to Cristina Ferraz Rigo for her minority reports.

Notes
1. See, for example,
www.elpais.com/articulo/semana/formas/agua/elpepuculbab/20080607elpbabese_3/Tes,
http://de.indymedia.org/2004/11/100052.shtml and http://zh2no.noblezabaturra.org/.
2. See Tjaco Walvis, 'Building Brand Locations', *Corporate Reputation Review*, Vol 5, No 4, 2003, pp 358–66, though Indymedia (see note 2) states that the Hanover Expo generated a significant deficit for the Expo itself.

Pelli Clarke Pelli

Cesar Pelli is best known for dramatic skyscrapers, like the Petronas Towers in Kuala Lumpur, and big urban complexes with vast glazed interior spaces, like Canary Wharf and the World Financial Center in Battery Park City. But his renamed firm, Pelli Clarke Pelli Architects, is now doing major hospitals and research centres, museums and concert halls, apartment houses, numerous college buildings – even airports. **Jayne Merkel** explains how he learnt to do memorable work of considerable complexity as she describes what Pelli Clarke Pelli is doing around the world.

Rafael Pelli, Fred W Clarke and Cesar Pelli in the Pelli Clarke Pelli New Haven office.

It is hard to imagine that the unprepossessing, three-storey, mixed-used block across Chapel Street from the oldest part of the Yale University campus could house a hundred people working on a quality and quantity of buildings unmatched anywhere else in America. A narrow entrance between two shops leads up to a sunny, first-floor lobby with conference rooms facing the street and a rather small studio at the rear. However, the studio leads to further studios on each side and in the adjacent buildings behind, one of which is several storeys. Still, all the spaces are modest in size. None seem corporate in any way. Only models of enormous buildings hint at the volume of work under way.

Pelli Clarke Pelli is designing the even larger Penn's Landing complex in Philadelphia, three towers for Porta Nuova in Milan, and a teaching hospital in Qatar, a flagship tower for a 17.4-hectare (43-acre) mixed-use development in Liverpool, Winnipeg International Airport, and college buildings at Yale, Grinnell, Southern Methodist, Duke and the universities of Texas and Illinois.

Cesar Pelli has received the American Institute of Architects (AIA) Gold Medal (in 1995) and 12 honorary degrees. His buildings have won every major design

Shanghai Pudong Lujiazui Comprehensive Development (with P&T Architects and ECADI), Lujiazui and Century Boulevards, Shanghai, China, due for completion 2010
This mixed-use development in the heart of the emerging Pudong district, between new mega-towers and older low-rise buildings, with views of the Huangpu River and the historic Bund, was the result of an invited international competition. Two gently angled towers, with occasional cuts, containing offices and hotels, will rise 250 and 260 metres (820.2 and 853 feet) from a four-storey podium with retail stores, restaurants and function spaces linked by tunnels and sky bridges. They will be surrounded by an extensively landscaped park with fountains, gardens, sitting areas and open courts leading to an underground cinema, stores, parking and connections to the subway.

award. Fred W Clarke, his long-time collaborator, has overseen numerous celebrated projects and lectured widely. His son, Rafael Pelli, has designed the most innovatively energy-efficient apartment buildings in America. Yet the firm is not constantly in the news. Their successes are taken for granted. And they concentrate their energies on designing well, instead of on public relations.

Born and educated in Tucumán in Argentina, Pelli moved to the US in 1952 to continue his studies at the University of Illinois. Two years later he joined Eero Saarinen and Associates in Bloomfield Hills, Michigan, and then moved to New Haven in 1961 with his family and most of his colleagues to continue Saarinen's work after the architect's tragic death at 51. The time Pelli spent with Saarinen significantly influenced his own practice. He learnt to choose his clients carefully, accept only those who want serious architecture, and not to take on more work than he can do well. He discovered the importance of sticking with a project until it was right, of finding the best talent around, and keeping his staff challenged. He pursued an interest in new technology, especially the reflective glass that Saarinen had developed, and in new ways to use technology creatively. And he learned, despite most practice at the time, the importance of making a building symbolic and specifically responsive to its site.

When the works Saarinen had designed were nearing completion in 1964, his practice was taken over by Kevin Roche and John Dinkeloo. Pelli moved to Los Angeles and joined the huge (700-strong) commercial architecture and engineering firm Daniel, Mann, Johnson and Mendenhall (DMJM) where the British architect Anthony Lumsden, who had also been at Saarinen's, was working. Pelli's first project there, Sunset Mountain Park, a huge residential complex in the Santa Monica Mountains, designed with Lumsden, won a *Progressive Architecture* (PA) award and appeared on the magazine's cover. Though it was never built, Sunset Mountain Park brought Pelli recognition at the firm, and he got to design the high-tech Teledyne Labs in Northridge, California (also with Lumsden) and the COMSAT Laboratory in Clarksberg, Maryland, as well as various office buildings and housing complexes.

In 1969, Pelli joined Victor Gruen Associates, the inventors of the now-ubiquitous enclosed suburban shopping mall, just as Gruen himself and his partner, Rudy Baumfeld, were retiring. Soon after he arrived, Pelli designed a winning competition scheme for UN City in Vienna, which employed the spine as a planning principal that was to become Pelli's hallmark. It was not built either, but, again, it led to choice projects. At Gruen, Pelli designed the Pacific Centre in Vancouver, the San Bernardino City Hall, the US Embassy in Tokyo (with Fred Clarke), the Rainbow Center Mall and Wintergarden in Niagara Falls, and the Pacific Design Center ('Blue Whale') in West Hollywood (1971–75), for which he designed a second (green) building in 1988 and is now adding a (red) one. He also did an attractive enclosed mall on the main street of downtown Columbus, Indiana, where Saarinen and a number of his office alumni had also received commissions from the architecture foundation of Saarinen's friend and client J Irwin Miller.

After five years at Gruen, transforming the firm's formulas for shopping malls into more ambitious urban projects, Pelli grew restless.

Cira Center (with Bower Lewis Thrower Architects), Philadelphia, Pennsylvania, 2005
This elegant, subtly twisted, crystalline 132.5-metre (435-foot) tall office tower beside Philadelphia's 30th Street Railroad Station is
the first of a proposed office and retail space complex near the universities. At this point, however, it stands alone on the west bank of
the Schuylkill River half a mile away, but is visible from the densely developed downtown area. Calibrated to change character from
different angles and at different times, the tower even has LED lights in its curtain wall to colour its surface for holidays and events.
Built on a platform over the rail yard, it has a light-filled foyer with a pedestrian sky bridge over the street to the train station.

**Petronas Towers (with KLCC Berhad Architectural Division),
Kuala Lumpur, Malaysia, 1997**
Pelli Clarke Pelli won the commission for the first phase of the
4.9-hectare (12.15-acre) Kuala Lumpur City with this scheme for
twin 88-storey towers, clad in stainless steel and connected by
a sky bridge on the 41st and 42nd floors. The geometry of the
towers, the corporate headquarters for the national petroleum
company, is based on Islamic traditions. The complex
incorporates Malaysian colours, patterns, traditions and crafts,
and includes a discovery centre, art gallery, Filharmonik hall,
conference centre, shopping and an entertainment galleria.

**Abandoibarra Masterplan and Torre Iberdrola
(with Aguinaga y Asociados and Balmori Associates), Bilbao,
Spain, due for completion 2011**
The Abandoibarra masterplan transforms an abandoned riverfront
industrial district between the Guggenheim Museum and the new
opera house, weaving new parkland and a mixed-use development
into the 19th-century Ensanche area. New private buildings are to
match the heights of the historic ones, but will reflect their own time.
At the river's edge, a 6-metre (19.7-foot) drop was replaced by smooth
pedestrian-friendly slopes with floodable and non-floodable walkways
(one walkway is for when it is flooded and the other is lower for
when it is not, so that both walkways can be used). The Torre
Iberdrola skyscraper, a softly rounded triangle in plan, tapers gently
towards the sky, suggesting a crystal obelisk. Its double skin will
provide panoramic views of the city and save energy.

Paradise Street Development Area, Liverpool, 2003
The large, retail-led, mixed-use Paradise Street development has areas of
varying character both in terms of scale and use. The central organising
element for the entire development is the 2-hectare (4.9-acre) Chavasse
Park, which is intended as a large-scale, delightful urban centrepiece.
Pelli Clarke Pelli is also designing the One Park West residential
development on the northwest corner of the park. The 380-unit, 13-
storey building will be a significant landmark on Liverpool's waterfront.

He received offers from the University of California Los Angeles and
Harvard, but chose to become Dean of the Yale School of
Architecture, so he moved back to New Haven, where he has lived
ever since. He founded Cesar Pelli & Associates in 1977 when he
was invited to expand the Museum of Modern Art in New York and
add a residential tower intended to defray operating expenses. The
56-storey building was Pelli's first skyscraper, an explicitly
contextual design with a subtly stepped-back top and geometric
pattern on its facades.

In the 1980s, Pelli's firm designed healthcare facilities for the
highly regarded Cleveland Clinic and St Luke's Episcopal Hospital in
Houston, as well as some huge office complexes – the Four Leaf
Towers and Four Oak, both in Houston, Four Stamford Forum in
Connecticut, and the 826,837.1-square-metre (8.9 million-square-
foot) World Financial Center at Battery Park City in New York. The last
project gave a sense of place to the landfill development next to the
historic Wall Street financial district. Its Canadian developers,
Olympia & York, later hired Pelli to design much of Canary Wharf, the
complex which led to their financial ruin.

When he left the deanship at Yale in 1985, even bigger and more
varied projects came Pelli's way: skyscrapers in Minneapolis,
Chicago, Los Angeles, Cleveland, Charlotte, San Francisco, and at
Canary Wharf; art centres in Charlotte, Cincinnati, Duluth and
Dayton; several more important hospitals; Washington DC's Reagan
National Airport; campus buildings for Rice, Princeton, Trinity, Wake
Forest, Vassar, the universities of Washington and Chicago, and
UCLA. He was well equipped to take on work like this. He had learnt
from the Los Angeles firms how to run an office efficiently, though he
preferred the studio atmosphere he had known at Saarinen's. He does
not take on more work than his senior people can personally oversee,
and associated firms produce contract documents for very large
projects. His masterplans had taught him how to organise big and
complicated public interior space, usually around a street-like spine.
And a serious amateur interest in science (he reads scientific journals
for fun) has helped him design complex facilities for medical
treatment and research.

When other architects of his generation were abandoning their
modern roots and embracing the historicising Postmodernism that
was sweeping the nation, Pelli saw no reason to follow one path or the
other. At Saarinen's office he had worked on the swooping, concrete,
bird-like TWA Terminal and the jagged towers of the Morse and Stiles
Colleges at Yale, which were made of concrete filled with rough
boulders and resembled an Italian hill town, a design intended to
relate to nearby collegiate Gothic structures in a contemporary way.
Similarly, Pelli used daring new reflective coloured-glass skins and
devised new shapes tailored to each particular site. Occasionally his
projects had vaguely classical forms, but these were simplified and
rendered in explicitly modern materials. Every building was different,
as in Saarinen's *oeuvre*. None looked quite like those of other
architects – or other Pelli buildings. His work never became branded
the way that of some of architecture's stars did. Still, major clients
flocked to him – and returned again and again.

International Finance Centre (with Rocco Design Limited), Hong Kong, China, 2002

The architects won the chance to design this northeast office tower and the southwest tower, half its size, on one of the most dramatic sites in the world, in an international competition. The complex also has a four-storey retail podium with a public roof garden and will eventually include a hotel and apartments. As an integral part of the new air terminal station with its express service to the Chek Lap Kok Airport, it is also a gateway to the city. The northeast tower tapers towards the top with carefully calculated setbacks. The curtain wall, clad in lightly reflective glass panels and silver pearl-toned mullions, shimmers like a pearl beside the narrowest crossing of Victoria Harbour, a fitting symbol for a city known as the 'Pearl of the Orient'.

**Porta Nuova and Porta Nuova Tower A, B, C
(with AAI Architects Inc and Tekne, Ingegneria), Milan,
Italy, due for completion 2010**

Currently under construction, this mixed-use development, north of the historic city centre on abandoned rail yards next to Garibaldi Station, is intended to serve as a gateway to the city and reconnect separated neighbourhoods. The architects developed the masterplan for the site and are designing the largest elements: a new public park, three curved-glass office towers and a podium with shops, restaurants and parking. To celebrate Milan's status as a fashion capital, there will be a Fashion Fiera at the southern end of the new park next to the larger, private development.

Daniel L Malone Engineering Center, Yale University, New Haven, Connecticut, 2005
Nestled into a difficult, triangular site, between a busy street and a nature trail on much lower ground, this unusually energy-efficient, six-storey structure manages to preserve the natural environment and respect nearby academic buildings. The main circulation corridor, cantilevered from the main structure and enclosed by a curved-glass curtain wall, creates a column-free space that admits natural light into all the work spaces behind it. A water-recycling system, high-performance glazing and a reflective white roof helped earn the building its gold LEED rating.

NHK Broadcasting Center, Osaka City Museum and Archaeological Resource Center, and Osaka National Museum of Art, Nakanoshima Island, Osaka, Japan, 1995–2001, 1996–2004
The 18-storey Broadcasting Center, clad in metal and highly reflective glass, rises beside the City Museum and Archaeological Resource Center, a 14-storey structure sheathed in granite on this small, historically important site next to the ruins of the ancient Naniwanomiya Palace on display inside. A concert hall for live broadcasts and recording occupies the lower floors of the taller tower. The contemporary art museum moved to the site later, and the three-level structure was built underground with a sculpturesque, lightweight stainless-steel entrance on the public plaza. To protect the galleries from the aqueous soil, the building is encased in concrete with a rubberised waterproofing membrane beneath the interior walls.

**Pacific Design Center and Expansion (with Gruen Associates),
West Hollywood, California, 1971–75, 1984–88, 2003–08**
The first building in this award-winning complex immediately
became a landmark, dubbed the 'Blue Whale' because of its shiny
blue glass skin, bulbous shape and bulk: 69,677.3 square metres
(750,000 square feet) on six floors. It has showrooms for interior
furnishings under a two-storey barrel-vaulted galleria. Then came
an angular building, sheathed in green spandrel glass, housing an
auditorium, amphitheatre, public plaza, exhibition gallery and
parking. Now, a pair of curved, red six- and eight-storey office
towers are adding 37,161.2 square metres (400,000 square feet) of
office space atop seven levels of parking.

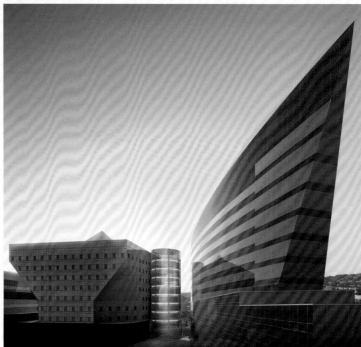

Visionaire Condominiums (with Shuman, Lichenstein, Claman, Efron), Battery Park City, New York, 2008

This 33-storey, 250-unit apartment tower, a few blocks south of Pelli's commanding World Financial Center, is the only residential building in the US to achieve the (highest) LEED platinum rating. It has a green, living roof and obtains 35 per cent of its electricity from renewable sources. Water from bathrooms and kitchens is filtered and pumped back for toilets. Located near the southern tip of Manhattan, the apartments have sweeping views of the Hudson River and New York cityscape. There is a children's playroom, spa, fitness centre, a sky-lit pool, and a roof garden on top of a 10-storey base which houses the Battery Park City Parks Conservancy.

In 1990, when the US was in recession, the Japanese began to hire foreign architects. Because he (and Clarke) had designed the US Embassy in Tokyo in 1972, Pelli was awarded the 30-storey NTT Headquarters there. This project led to a masterplan for Fukuoka, the 139,354.6-square-metre (1.5 million-square-foot) Sea Hawk Hotel there, and the 994,062.5-square-metre (10.7 million-square-foot) Petronas Towers in Kuala Lumpur, which were briefly the tallest buildings in the world – and instant icons. These, of course, led to other major Asian projects – in Tokyo, Hong Kong and Osaka – as well as projects in Bilbao and Buenos Aires. Now there are also major ones in Shanghai, Beijing, Madrid, Seville, Milan, Liverpool, Hong Kong, Las Vegas, Boston, San Francisco, Santiago, Mexico City, Abu Dhabai and Doha, Qatar.

The architects are also busy closer to home. Rafael Pelli, who worked briefly for his father after he graduated from Yale in 1979, returned 10 years later after architecture school at Harvard and a stint with Hardy Holzman Pfeiffer. He is now in charge of Pelli Clarke Pelli's New York office in an old Garment District building, near the Chelsea art galleries, where a couple of dozen architects are doing mostly high-rise residential and collegiate work. In 2003 he completed the Solaire, the first officially 'green' (LEED gold) apartment tower in New York, and is now an authority on energy-efficient design. (LEED is the Leadership in Energy and Environmental Design Green Building Rating System of a the US Green Building Council.) Pelli Clarke Pelli's New York office is currently completing another pioneering residential tower in Battery Park City, the Visionaire, and working on several others, each different from the next, in other parts of the city and Washington, DC.

In New Haven, Cesar Pelli and Fred Clarke have done half a dozen buildings on Yale's distinguished campus and a downtown office tower, and are designing a citywide Humanities High School. Several years ago, the university hired a famous American firm that was working at the medical school to design a new biology building on Science Hill, near Philip Johnson's Kline Biology Tower. Pelli, meanwhile, was doing the Malone Engineering Center on an impossible corner site nearby, with heavy traffic and a 6-metre (19.7-foot) drop from the sidewalk to a wooded passage below. He solved the problem intelligently and elegantly, while things were not going so well for the other architects on the medical campus. Before you knew it, Pelli Clarke Pelli was asked to take on the important biology building.

This incident may have been unique, but it was also typical. These architects are consummate professionals. They work very hard (and quietly) to make buildings that are not only beautiful, but also stimulating, functional, original, appropriate and technologically advanced. Δ+

Saatchi Gallery/Duke of York Headquarters

Paul Davis + Partners for Cadogan Estates, Saatchi Gallery/Duke of York Headquarters, Chelsea, London, 2008
Despite the multiplicity of changes throughout the building's long life, very little has changed externally, and modifications to the structure are primarily interior.

The new rear extension and glazed link have brought external walls inside the building. The contrast between new and old, and the way the different architectures overlap, was the result of considerable thought by Paul Davis + Partners.

The glazed link between original building and extension was the result of a highly detailed discussion with English Heritage. The palette of materials is uncompromisingly modern, although the composition has been drawn from the historic buildings on the wider Cadogan estate.

The Duke of York Headquarters in Chelsea, London, has undergone a major rehabilitation. For many years its fine Georgian facade had belied a run-down and messed-about interior, inhabited by the offices of the Ministry of Defence. **David Littlefield** describes how, under the stewardship of the Cadogan Estate and Paul Davis + Partners, this historic structure is now reasserting its dignity, while also accommodating a series of bespoke gallery spaces.

Sloane Square's Duke of York Headquarters is about to enter a radically new chapter of its life. The transformation from an army headquarters to Charles Saatchi's art gallery does not sound quite as dramatic as Tate Modern's reinvention of a power station, but this functional leap is certainly of that order. The Ministry of Defence was merely an inhabitant of this building, rather than a custodian, and everything about its postwar interior fit-out was either brutally functional or cringingly tasteless – and very often both. What Paul Davis + Partners have done, more than anything else, is give this building back a little dignity.

Built early in the 19th century, this large classical edifice (designed by John Sanders, a pupil of Sir John Soane) was originally built as a boarding school for the sons and daughters of soldiers. In the Edwardian era the building became a military administration centre, hosting the head offices of the Territorial Army and eventually providing space for a handful of other units, including the Parachute Regiment and the SAS. During its entire life, this building has been rather mercilessly pushed around, and there was even a point when the architects wondered whether a facade-retention job (involving the demolition and reconstruction of everything behind) was an appropriate response.

'What surprised us was how much abuse the building had taken. It really had been knocked about,' says project architect and practice partner Alec Howard. Columns had to be inserted at a relatively early phase in the building's life to compensate for structural inadequacies, while double-height rooms on the first floor were later remade as separate single-storey spaces. Since the 1950s doorways had become filled in, fireplaces had been removed, partitions put up and a polite dry lining installed to disguise the riot of brickwork scars beneath. Very often the partitioning was plain clumsy, and purely decorative fireplaces bore no relation to the position of chimneys. Despite the natural strength of the building, Howard's team had to give it 'the kiss of life'.

The recent history of the Duke of York Headquarters has been no less complex. Although the army vacated the building in 2005, Paul Davis + Partners were asked by Cadogan Estates, owners of the site on which the building sits, to take a look at it as early as 1999. Back then the assumption was that the vast rooms would make ideal open-plan offices, but a slump in the commercial

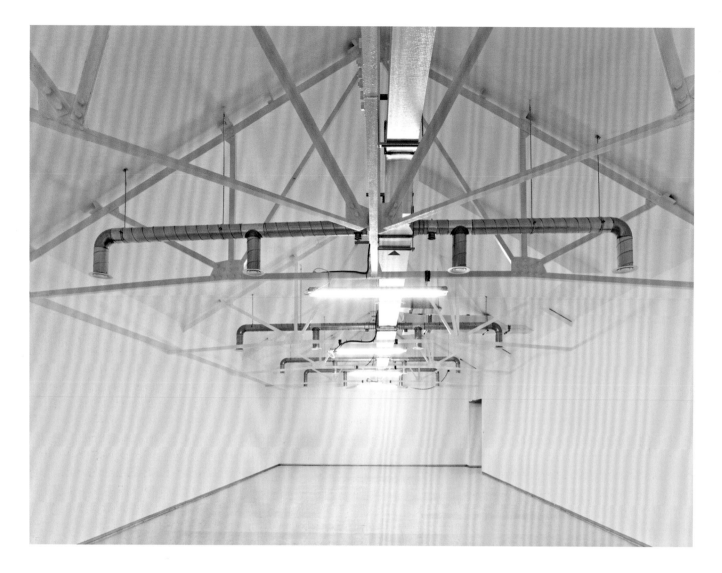

above: The upper galleries of the building are animated by the exposed roof structure – steelwork fitted after the Second World War to replace timbers that were destroyed in a bomb attack. The industrial aesthetic of these upper galleries is reminiscent of Saatchi's original gallery on north London's Boundary Road.

right top: The 1801 ground plan of the Duke of York Headquarters, showing architect John Sanders' symmetrical room plan. The building was built as a school for the children of soldiers, and adapted for army administration in the early 20th century. A recent conversion, involving the replacement of the rear extension with a larger volume, has recreated the building as an art gallery for Charles Saatchi.

right bottom: Ground-floor plan of the Duke of York Headquarters as reworked for the Saatchi Gallery. The four large volumes, once classrooms, have been reinstated, and the rear extension has been replaced by a larger structure.

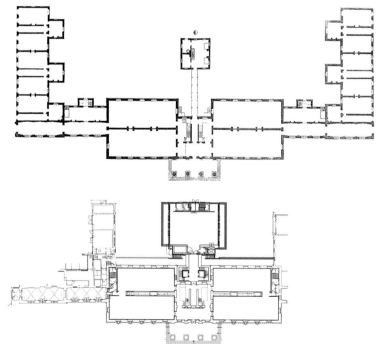

market around 2002 forced architects and owners to think again. For a while it looked like Sotheby's would convert the building to an auction house, but eventually, in 2005, Cadogan struck a deal with Charles Saatchi who was moving his art collection out of London's County Hall. Significantly, the owner–occupier relationship has meant two architectural firms working on the building: Paul Davis + Partners have acted for Cadogan, while Allford Hall Monaghan Morris (AHMM) have worked for Saatchi.

As Cadogan wants to retain control over its considerable estate, it will never allow a tenant the freedom to develop one of its buildings with their own architect. Paul Davis + Partners has therefore worked directly for the estate owner while bearing the needs of Saatchi in mind. In fact, the practice has already set the design standard for much of the immediate neighbourhood: the adjacent Duke of York Square development, including the new retail units and listed-building conversions, are all Paul Davis' work, as is the reinvention of the nearby Cadogan Hall and other buildings in Sloane Square. The Duke of York Headquarters, especially the new stone-and-glass extension at the rear, deliberately speaks the same architectural language as everything around it, which gives the entire district a certain consistency. 'Cadogan is quite interesting in that it doesn't take a separate building approach to development; it's more of an estate-wide view,' says Alec Howard. 'They've never taken the view that they're just rent collectors. They have a very long-term perspective on things.' Contact with AHMM has obviously been considerable, however, and this article was written more or less at the point at which the project passed from one architect to the other.

There was a moment during the project when the entire building was revealed, and the strength and immensity of the place became clear: the thickness of its walls, its textures and raw dimensions, the scars of the many (generally thoughtless) interventions and the few original decorative elements. Stripped of its cellular offices and other compartments it became obvious how the main spaces, which had once been classrooms, had each accommodated 250 children. In anthropomorphic terms, the building was lying in casualty; once made secure, hard decisions had to be taken about its rehabilitation. The result was a combination of bold intervention and careful restoration. After an incendiary bombing in the Second World War, the timber-and-slate roof had been replaced with one of steel and clay tiles painted black; the steelwork remains, but the slate has returned. Long-hidden doors have been reinstated and the original circulation restored. The basement was excavated, underpinned and supplied with windows to create decent office and storage space. A

new extension of glass and lightweight stone cladding (thin veneers of stone on a metallic honeycomb structure) has replaced a smaller building at the rear, English Heritage having been convinced, correctly, that the old and the new would touch each other only lightly. By and large, the original stairs survive unaltered, while painted timber panelling has been installed to replace a long-lost and only guessed-at original feature. The brickwork, especially where external walls have been brought inside thanks to the glazed link to the extension, have not been scrubbed up too much.

One curiosity along the slow march towards the building's rescue was Charles Saatchi's determination to create 'white cube' spaces for the presentation of his artworks. He wanted artificial lighting, rather than daylight, and most of the very large windows that characterise the building had to be somehow dispensed with. English Heritage suggested covering the glass with film, but Davis and Howard took the view that this was too simple – that the application of a film would merely convert the windows into two-dimensional surfaces. Instead, they took some inspiration from the window displays of department stores, which manage to retain the spatial depth of glass while effectively sealing off the interior from the outside. The windows now open on to grey boxes as deep as the wall, sustaining the sense that there is space beyond the glass. The technique works rather well, and it is only when the sun is shining directly on to the facade that the technique is revealed through giveaway shadows. This is a shame, though, and one cannot help wondering why artworks that were undoubtedly conceived with the help of natural light have to be displayed without it. The building ends up with two personalities – the external appearance of brick and windows, and the internal spaces of featureless white surfaces. It will be interesting to see how many gallery visitors notice the difference. Interestingly, the galleries in the new extension (including a very large double-height space overlooked by a mezzanine balcony) are provided with windows.

At the time of writing, there were still a number of uncertainties regarding how the Saatchi/AHMM team would handle the building as presented by Paul Davis + Partners. Saatchi was, for example, considering squaring off the original arched doorways. Surely there are only so many changes one can make to a building before one has to ask whether one has found the right property? That said, a wonderful floor of 9-metre (29.5-foot) timber lengths has been laid to AHMM's specification, while the lighting and stretched-fabric ceilings promise to be elegant. After surviving two centuries of the rough and tumble of history, Cadogan and Paul Davis + Partners have ensured this building can survive a good deal longer. ⚙+

David Littlefield is an architectural writer. He has written and edited a number of books, including *Architectural Voices: Listening to Old Buildings*, published by John Wiley & Sons (October 2007). He is also curating the exhibition 'Unseen Hands: 100 Years of Structural Engineering', which will run at the Victoria & Albert Museum until 7 September 2008. He has taught at Chelsea College of Art & Design and the University of Bath.

Beyond White Walls

With the strictures of Modernism behind us, the possibilities of ornament are being rediscovered, but often in a vacuum without method or understanding. **Oliver Domeisen** describes how in diploma units at the Architectural Association in London ornament is being pursued with a purpose as contemporary digital design and construction techniques are fused with an awareness of grammar and definition.

Alex Kaiser (AA Diploma Unit 13), A New Ornament for the Architectural Association, Bedford Square, London, 2007/08

opposite: The curvilinear dynamics of a new ornamental language drawn from the Rococo engulf the entrance of the AA. Elements of the Georgian square, such as cast-iron railings and the stone paving, are drawn into the building and combine with aluminium bronze mullions and concrete partitions to form a spectacle of transformation.

left: The intersection of two programmatically distinct spaces within the AA is marked by ornamental intricacy and intensity. Ornament here does not only frame the opening in the partition wall, but facilitates a seamless moment of transition that invites new forms of occupation.

Do you not see the greatness of our age resides in our very inability to create new ornament? We have gone beyond ornament, we have achieved plain, undecorated simplicity. Behold, the time is at hand, fulfilment awaits us. Soon the streets of the cities will shine like white walls.

— Adolf Loos, *Ornament and Crime*, 1908[1]

A century after Loos' polemic condemned ornament to the fringes of the discourse, we are witnessing a return to the elaborate eloquence of an architectural idiom that allows for a building to talk to us about more than its own existence. Contemporary practice, if not theory, increasingly seems to abandon the autistic silence of Modernism and enters into a dialogue with today's capitalist cultures of representation and societal trends towards individual expression. The lost language of ornament is being rediscovered as architecture's intrinsic mode of communication. But while digital design and production methods can compensate for lost craft skills in the creation of figurative intricacy and mass-customised form, the choice of motifs and distribution of ornament upon the structure as a whole often remains arbitrary and confused. Our cities may no longer shine like white walls, but flicker like television sets, and our buildings often remain not 'comely in the nude'[2] but badly dressed. It is within this context that, for the last two years, our research at the Architectural Association (AA) into the history, theory and practice of architectural ornament has been situated. Students of Intermediate Unit 9 (2006/07) and Diploma Unit 13 (2007/08) have created ornamental languages that project past principles and definitions of ornament into a fundamentally altered state of architectural design and construction.

The Grammar of Ornament

To even consider a new grammar of ornament we must understand its manifold functions and powers, which could be summarised thus: Ornament can occur at any scale as linear motif, surface decoration or object. It tends to lead a marginal existence located in-between things. Traditionally ornament would be found on the keystone of the arch, in the capital of the column, concealing joints of walls and ceilings and framing doors and windows. In picture frames and in the border of the illuminated manuscript, ornament negotiates between the real world outside and the fictional world of the text or painting. Ornament is containment. It is the home of metamorphosis uniting and transforming conflicting worldly elements. It is an image of combination and a spectacle of transformation. Ornament is a method to subsume almost anything into the architectural idiom: human bodies, plants, militaria, geometric patterns, fantastical beasts – it is the realm of monsters and hybrids. Ornament is transgressive. It sits comfortably between realism and abstraction, antiquity and modernity, mechanical objectivity and artistic subjectivity, convention and expression, and the real and the ideal. Ornament operates trans-historically and trans-culturally. It is constant dynamic movement and expansion. Ornament is not truth – it is mimesis, material transubstantiation, deception, artifice, pleasure and beauty that render utility acceptable. Ornament is distributed upon objects to provide a vision or world picture that is absent in the mere expression of utility. All ornament is decorative, but not all decoration is ornament. Ornament exists beyond the rules of decorum. It possesses visual, sensual and perceptual significance as well as functional, historical and social meaning. Heinrich Wölfflin (*Prolegomena to a Psychology of Architecture*, 1886) saw ornament as the expression of architecture's forceful will to manifest a society's *Formgefühl* (sense of form), encapsulating its Zeitgeist in ever changing formulations. Ornament is a sign of its time.

Lines of Beauty

In his 2007/08 project for an ornamental reconfiguration of the late 18th-century home of the AA on London's Georgian Bedford Square, Diploma Unit 13 student Alex Kaiser employs the curvaceous dynamics of Rococo geometry. Based on William Hogarth's Line of Beauty (a conical sinus curve), various architectural elements are subjected to material and geometric transformations. Intricate configurations of C- and S-scrolls, the constituents of the Rocaille, are strategically placed at interstitial moments within the building, such as the entrance, a window or an internal partition. Following ornamental traditions these sinuous convolutions at once

mark and conceal the joints between distinct elements, be they spatial, tectonic or programmatic. As in the Rococo, Kaiser's seemingly animated swirls and cartouches create dynamic inversions that liberate themselves from elements of structure and invade elements of space, portraying metamorphosis as a gradual process. The result is an ornamental language that produces aesthetic coherence and contextual continuity without homogeneity. As a tool of differentiation, the ornament here creates moments of visual and functional intensity. It unifies disparate elements such as cast-iron railings, aluminium bronze mullions and window frames, seating, cable ducts and brackets into a seamless whole of dancing lines and twisting surfaces. The ornamentation occurs at various scales; it is manifest in the curvature of a structural concrete wall as well as in the minute engravings of the glazing. It oscillates between surface pattern and sculptural object. Ultimately these ornamental interventions, concentrated and momentary as they are, facilitate a dialogue between the AA and its Neoclassical neighbours, between the internalised academic realm and the external urban reality, and among discrete entities within the school.

Anthropomorphic Iconography

AA Intermediate Unit 9 student Amandine Kastler (winner of the RIBA Bronze Medal in 2007) designed an extension to the Victoria & Albert Museum, located within its courtyard, that serves as a facility to house the figurative marble and sacred silver collections currently stored off-site. Ornament is used to communicate the intended purpose and content of the building in the same manner in which the statues of saints adorning the facades of Gothic cathedrals would speak about the buildings' intended nature. Kastler further sets out to integrate the structure with the anthropomorphism of the objects it houses. The newly constructed architectural body rests in the tradition of atlases and caryatids (structural metaphors in human form), but discards the ideal body of classicism and embraces a contemporary,

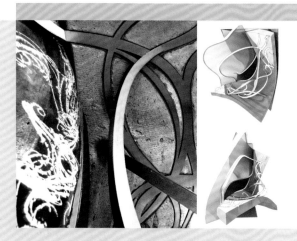

Window detail prototype (concrete, aluminium bronze and glass). The ornamental scrollwork unifies different architectural elements such as structural walls, window frames, brackets and glazing. The vocabulary of ornament ranges from metal inlay and concrete relief to three-dimensional objects and text engraved on glass. The geometric principles of curvature and bifurcation allow for multidirectional expansion across scales.

Johann Esaias Nilson, *New Coffee House (Neues Caffehaus)*, Augsburg, 1756
The invasive ornament of the Rococo – the Rocaille – is an amalgamation of nature and artifice. It transmogrifies everything it touches into a seamless, ever expanding space of asymmetrical dynamics and material transubstantiation.

A fleshy mound of muscular white marble rises from the V&A's quadrangle, topped by a shroud of perforated flayed skin. The container reveals through its ornamentation what it conceals.

Amandine Kastler (AA Intermediate Unit 9), A Cabinet of Curiosities, Victoria & Albert Museum, London, 2006/07
Cladding detail prototype (Carrara marble and Corten steel). Two different material systems, one structural, the other cladding, are joined by a system of embossed or CNC-milled veins. Anthropomorphic iconography becomes the pervading ornamental principle that stiffens the steel panels and channels rainwater across the marble surface.

more amorphous and distended physicality. The perfectly proportioned shapes of Greco-Roman sculpture rest within a cavernous mass of bulging marble that forms vaulted mounds of veined petrified muscle within the museum's courtyard. Elevated above is a shrine containing the sacred silver objects. This smaller space, perforated by an oculus that opens to the sky, is shrouded in a perforated, rusting skin of Corten steel reflecting the iconography of the flayed religious body. Expanding across both surfaces – those of structural marble and steel cladding – is a system of continuous bifurcating veining. Convex and concave veins facilitate hidden joints and channels for lighting and services, as well as drainage and controlled patination by directing rainwater (and rust) over the marble surfaces. The critique of the museum is twofold: its stated aim of eternal preservation is questioned by introducing an ornamental choreography of ageing and material deterioration, and the white-cube gallery space is abandoned in favour of a contextual ornamentation, an environment that engages eloquently with the exhibits.

Both of the projects here demonstrate that a meaningful future for architectural ornament can only emerge from combining contemporary possibilities of design and construction with an understanding of its history and theory. To again quote Louis Sullivan (*Ornament in Architecture*. 1892): 'The possibilities of ornamentation, so considered, are marvellous; and before us open, as a vista, conception so rich, so varied, so poetic, so inexhaustible, that the mind pauses in its flight and life indeed seems but a span.'[3] Δ+

Oliver Domeisen produces, teaches, curates and writes about architecture. He studied at the ETH Zurich and the Architectural Association (AA), London. He was an AA Unit Master for Intermediate Unit 9 from 2001 to 2007, and is currently a Unit Master for Diploma Unit 13. He was also AAVSP Master from 2005 to 2007. A project architect in Zaha Hadid's office from 1997 to 2000, he is now the director of dlm architectural designers ltd. He was the curator of the recent 'Re-sampling Ornament' exhibition at the Swiss Architecture Museum (June to September 2008).

'Unit Factor' is edited by Michael Weinstock, who is Academic Head and Master of Technical Studies at the Architectural Association School of Architecture in London. He is co-guest-editor with Michael Hensel and Achim Menges of the *Emergence: Morphogenetic Design Strategies* (May 2004) and *Techniques and Technologies in Morphogenetic Design* (March 2006) issues of *Architectural Design*. He is currently writing a book on the architecture of emergence for John Wiley & Sons Ltd.

Notes
1. From Adolf Loos, *Ornament and Crime: Selected Essays*, Ariadne Press (California), 1997.
2. '… I should say that it would be greatly for our aesthethic good if we should refrain entirely from the use of ornament for the period of years, in order that our thought might concentrate acutely upon the production of buildings well formed and comely in the nude.' Louis Sullivan, *Ornament in Architecture*, 1892. From *Kindergarten Chats and Other Writings*, Schulz (New York), 1947, p 187.
3. Ibid, p 190.

Getting Wet About Urban Design

Neil Spiller is thrilled by IwamotoScott's Hydro-Net – a futuristic design proposal for San Francisco that thinks about water in an entirely new way.

From the outside, at least, it is a popular conception that Americans are blithely in denial about global warming. It seems that a total reliance on market dynamics cannot deliver the necessary solutions to mitigate massive ecological damage. Messing about trading carbon quotas seems to me to be as useful as the proverbial 'urination in the wind'. What is needed is some holistic and original thinking about city infrastructure projects, in effect 'blue sky' cities.

The architectural avant-garde has steered clear of the utopian city since the early 1970s; it was a casualty of the oil crisis, 'winters of discontent' and the cooling of 'the white heat of technology' as the hippie hangover gripped previously frivolous young architects. Consequently, little polemic and experimental city design has occurred in the last 30 years. Architects have concentrated on one-off bespoke iconic building at the expense of a city's systematics and connectivity.

So it is great to see a young, talented and American firm of architects positing a thoughtful, polemic relook at the city infrastructure of San Francisco and driving that proposition with water – its availability, its threat and its delight. In January 2008, the History Channel ran a competition to visualise the San Francisco of a hundred years hence. IwamotoScott Architecture's winning Hydro-Net project proposes that the new city be interconnected in all manner of different ways, with, for example, hydrogen-fuelled hover cars buzzing at high speed at high level. The city thus emerges above ground at the coast of the bay and opportunistic built nodes take advantage of fortuitous juxtapositions of topology, infrastructure and functional need. This is all relatively normal. What is original is IwamotoScott's thinking about water in many of its forms.

Hydro-Net also serves to simultaneously collect, distribute and store fresh water, geothermal energy and hydrogen fuel. Built with automated drilling robots, its tunnel walls are structured using carbon nano-tube technology. Algae ponds will reoccupy areas along the bay,

IwamotoScott Architecture, Hydro-Net, San Francisco, California, 2008
View from the Bay on a foggy day – a new urban morphology instantly recognisable as San Francisco.

Sinuous towers filled with algae punctuate the urban topology of San Francisco.

Model delineating both above- and below-ground networks with an almost fungal mycelium aesthetic.

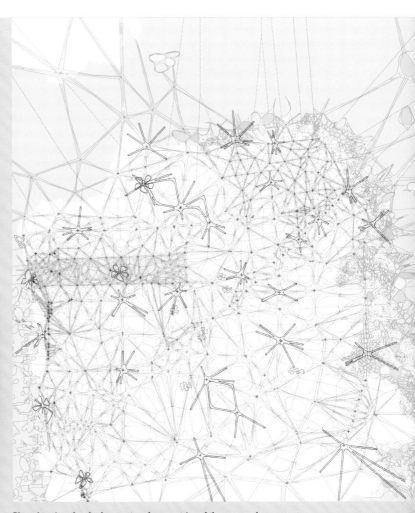

Plan showing the deployment and geometries of the proposal.

impacted by the projected 5-metre (16.4-foot) water-level rise of global climate change. This new aquaculture zone provides the raw material for the production of hydrogen fuel that is stored and distributed within the nano-tube tunnel walls. New high-density housing coexists with this aquaculture zone as a forest of sinuous towers. Hydro-Net thus becomes a device to tap the vast reserves of water and power housed within the earth below San Francisco, storing and distributing energy and fresh water from existing underground geothermal fields and aquifers stretching from Golden Gate Park to the airport. Replacing today's street paving which sends rainwater run-off into the sewer with new porous pavements that allow rain to recharge the aquifers, Hydro-Net also links to an array of fog harvesters, creating diversified sources of water.

Ultimately, Hydro-Net sponsors new programmatic potentials in its under ground nodes and above-ground tendrils, while allowing much of the character of above-ground San Francisco to be preserved and evolve organically. It was created in just a week, and is an

illustration of how architects, with their broad education, can swiftly develop thoughts and ideas that can make a critical contribution to the sustainable city debate – a contribution that is often missing from the output of hundreds of urban and city planning courses worldwide.

Virtuality and digital design have had a massive effect on the language of architecture, but they are seldom translated into humanity's largest artefact – the city. City planners are often still deeply set on methods, processes and ideologies that have been shown time and time again to be unsuccessful, except for a wealthy minority. The ubiquitous models of town planning need to be turned on their heads in favour of the sustainable urban opportunities that can be found within the uniqueness of each city – its topology, its climate, its seasonal variation and its specialisations – which, after all, is how older cities formed in the first place. Digital techniques and processes can help us visualise and propose ecological solutions. Here's to IwamotoScott, the first of many I hope. ᴆ+

Neil Spiller is Professor of Architecture and Digital Theory and Vice Dean at the Bartlett, University College London.

Horizons of User-Centred Design

Valentina Croci outlines how the new focus on the user in new technologies and human–computer interaction is moving towards 'cognitive engineering'. This puts less emphasis on the actual hardware and more on who uses it and how technology can give new meaning to our daily lives, as well as relevant computer interfaces.

Philips Research, Atmosphere Flipbook, 2007
The device allows for variations in the colour of the lighting in a space using a tactile interface that is as simple to use as a photo album. It is part of a larger project that includes Intelligent Lighting Tiles, a series of LED tiles that offer varying colours and patterns, and the Reactive Spotlight, a shop-window lighting system that changes the intensity of the light as customers approach the merchandise on display.

William Gaver (Department of Design, Goldsmiths College, University of London), Jan Humble (University of Nottingham) and Nicholas Villar and Alex Wilkie (Lancaster University), Local Barometer, 2008
The device is composed of an online display that shows images and texts relative to activities near the user's home, and reveals the sociocultural context of the surrounding area. It uses postal code reader software to collect a list of postal codes in a given area, with the span of the area it is capable of detecting dependent on the speed and direction of the wind. Web-ripping software uses the postal codes to extract content from the selected sites.

The design of computer and electronic instruments is becoming more focused on the user's point of view and methods of using technology. In April 2008, the Computer/Human Interaction (CHI) Conference, the most important international annual event dealing with the theme of human–computer interaction (HCI), presented a shift in the computational contents of such instruments and the context in which interaction takes place. Interest has moved from *what* we can do with technology, to *how* we can do it, concentrating on the user, the environment and interpersonal relations. This involves not only the design of new types of digital device, but also a degree of theoretical contamination as sociology and humanist disciplines enter into the world of information sciences and we move towards 'cognitive engineering'.

The parameters that define the social context (for example, class, environment, race or gender) contribute to establishing the rituals of using technological instruments and redefining, as a consequence, the interfaces and software. Microsoft's Bill Buxton underlines how the primary change in computer design must not lie in the hardware of the machines, but in those who use them and why.[1] In fact, the technological innovation of electronic and digital instruments has not been met by an equal transformation in the habits of their users. In order to introduce something innovative in the users' experience it is necessary to identify new meanings for available technologies. Buxton hopes for a transformation that will lead to the design of a 'generative' activity that creates finite products, and an 'evaluative' process that produces more flexible instruments capable of matching human behaviour. Computer design requires a more interdisciplinary approach and must be tied to product design.

The value of HCI experiences is pursued by the Department of Design at Goldsmiths College at the University of London. The Threshold Devices created by William Gaver's group are 'affective media', focused on integrating, or giving a new meaning to, existing electronic and digital instruments. These objects connect information, for example from the web, with the physical context in which we find ourselves. The Local Barometer uses postal codes for the online collection of information related to a specific area of reference, while the Plane Tracker reproduces the destinations of airline flights on a screen in residences near airports. These are not Second Life 3-D virtual world style simulations, but instruments that enrich the experience of the domestic environment and offer a greater awareness of that which takes place around us. What is also interesting about these two devices is their layout, which is more akin to traditional home appliances than to the latest generation of electronic instruments, and responds to the need to provide a new language of form for information technologies that are already present in the home.

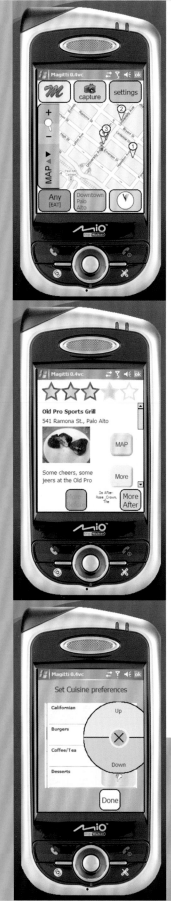

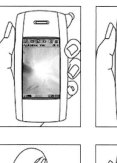

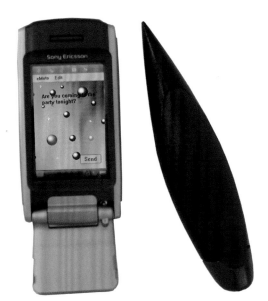

Kristina Höök, Anna Ståhl, Petra Sundström and Jarmo Laaksolahti, eMoto, Mobile Life Centre, University of Stockholm and Swedish Institute of Computer Science, Kista, Stockholm, 2008
eMoto is a text-messaging software that allows the user to choose the background display that accompanies his or her text in order to communicate their mood, giving the message contents an emotional quality and enriching communication.

The user composes the background display based on codes of reference established between one or more users. He or she defines the meaning of the message, as the device does not automatically couple background and mood.

Palo Alto Research Center (PARC), Magitti Mobile Leisure Guide, 2008
Connected to Geotagging and GPS environmental systems, and the on-line community, the Magitti system filters the information available from these to provide real-time information about leisure activities, such as dining, shopping or clubbing, in the user's local area. The system learns the user's preferences (based on past behaviour) in order to make a selection of local offerings. Its interface and functions are based on interviews that reveal social practices in urban spaces, and operation is similar to that of a mobile phone, requiring only one hand.

William Gaver (Department of Design, Goldsmiths College, University of London), Jan Humble (University of Nottingham) and Nicholas Villar and Alex Wilkie (Lancaster University), Plane Tracker, 2008
The Plane Tracker is a freestanding, polyhedral cabinet fitted with a screen. The system decodes radio signals from passing aircraft and translates them into geographical locations using GoogleEarth maps. The latter information allows the software to create images relating to flight conditions, routes or destinations. The aim of Plane Tracker is to create narrations using technological devices, helping to create an appreciation of the possible connections between where one lives and the rest of the world. The form of the device recalls the aesthetic of the 1950s, at the beginning of the 'jet age', and makes reference to the foot of Charles and Ray Eames' chaise longue of 1948.

The Philips Research Unit, based in the Netherlands, designs electronic and digital appliances for a wide range of uses – from communication to well-being and medical assistance, to tools of pervasive computing for the home. A common element resides in the desire to give new meaning to our daily practices and routines. This means that the consumer electronics sector need not produce universal instruments, but ones that can be adapted to users in different cultural contexts. The examples presented here place the accent on common practices: interaction with traditional home furnishings and the variation of environmental parameters, such as the colour and intensity of light. These instruments stimulate our choices through direct and natural interaction. It is thus the electronic device that adapts to the environment and not the user.

The search for involvement, as well as enjoyment, through interaction with the device is common to many prototypes and new mobile communications software. Graphic interfaces tend to be more intuitive, with less functions and control menus, allowing for a different form of user engagement, based less on the performance of the device and more on the possibilities of social relations that it makes possible. This is the intent of the mobile-phone software prototypes Connecto, developed by the Departments of Computer Science at the universities of San Diego and Glasgow, and the Magitti Mobile Leisure Guide, developed by the Palo Alto Research Center (PARC) in California. The first uses GSM technology to track the position of the phone and find information about the space in which it is located to provide the user with information. The second is a sort of guide that provides real-time information about activities in the area, based on a search that matches the user's preferences. These devices also accommodate different levels of computer skills, allowing for a degree of personalisation and intuitive interaction without requiring the user to be a computer expert. Both prototypes also allow for the construction of 'personal geographies' that can be shared with others using a community-based language.

Display language is also a focus of the eMoto project developed by the University of Stockholm's Mobile Life Centre. This device uses text-messaging software to communicate the user's mood via the composition of the screen background, adding an emotional element to traditional instruments of communication and facilitating the construction of expressive codes between interlocutors. The user chooses the colours and defines their meaning, thus the design of the graphic interfaces is also based on developments in the fields of semiotics and sociology.

Information programming is also focused on the following: the methods by which it becomes an everyday device, fundamental to social dynamics, the sharing of experiences with users and the fruition of built space. Given that the electronic device remains an important element of intermediation in social rituals, it is necessary that the design considers any possible side effects such as 'microbugging' or violations of privacy between users. Above all, it is important that the contents of the application are powerful, in order to ensure that we do not lose our sense of the everyday once the novelty of the device has worn off. Δ+

Translated from the Italian version into English by Paul David Blackmore.

Valentina Croci is a freelance journalist of industrial design and architecture. She graduated from Venice University of Architecture (IUAV), and attained an MSc in architectural history from the Bartlett School of Architecture, London. She achieved a PhD in industrial design sciences at the IUAV with a theoretical thesis on wearable digital technologies.

Note
1. Bill Buxton, *Sketching User Experience*, Morgan Kauffman (San Francisco), 2008.

Kiss and Cathcart Architects, New York Sunworks and Arup, Design for a Vertically Integrated Greenhouse, 2008
Views of a vertical integrated greenhouse in a café. The purpose-built roof structure allows multi-level growing of fast-maturing salads and vegetables.

Building Integrated Food Production

Ken Yeang combines forces with **Michael Guerra**, author of *The Edible Container Gardener*, to make the compelling case for the integration of space and facilities for food production in new and refurbished buildings.

Food access is critical to human sustainability. It is, however, currently threatened by many different forces. These range from local problems such as poorly conceived development on previously fertile land, to wider global tendencies, such as the current rush for biofuels and our increasing dependency on oil for the production, processing and transportation of food. While developed nations exercise their economic and political clout to maintain their access to imported foods, 862 million people are facing starvation;[1] some of these populations are living in the very same countries that are exporting food to the West. It is a situation that is further exacerbated by increasing oil consumption and urbanisation that puts greater distance between food and its consumers, further fast-forwarding the end of oil resources. The combined dependence on fossil fuels and distance from a local food supply provides the underlying mechanisms for climate change, desertification and the increasing loss of fertility that, in turn, puts further pressure on any remaining productive land.

Even before anyone gets in their car to drive to the out-of-town supermarket, oil is used in food production and distribution for ploughing, pesticides, fertilisers, harvesting, processing, packaging and transport. Such is our dependence on a dwindling oil supply that major world cities like London are never more than five days from starvation. The cost of the entire food production and consumption cycle has become so inflated that the price of a typical lettuce bought in a supermarket is often about a pound, whereas 1,000 lettuce seeds can be bought for approximately the same amount. For a city to survive in a post-oil economy it is imperative that food is sourced from within a few metres, rather than from

thousands of miles away. Building Integrated Food Production (BIFP) is being developed as a reaction to the loss of productive land to property development and the pressure to reduce food transportation, while also recognising the considerable synergies that can be realised when food production is brought within, and around, the structures where we live and work.

Awareness of these issues has driven some city dwellers to take street-level action. In London and other developed cities around the world there has been a grass-roots reaction to the lack of available growing space, most conspicuously publicised through the 'guerilla gardener' movement.[2] Most significantly, food is now being grown on balconies, in front gardens and in small micro-farms that feed their produce into boxed vegetable schemes. There are 17 city farms and 100 community gardens in London alone.[3] In Cuba, where the loss of subsidised Soviet oil has had an immediate impact on the local economy, public parks and empty building lots are being turned to productive use with help from the state.

Planners, developers and architects hold the key to a city's sustainability. Many architectural practices have been developing ideas for sustainable structures capable of generating their own electricity, heat and light, and harvesting their own rainwater for decades.[4] (In this issue alone there are two further articles that integrate plants with buildings – see 'Living Buildings' and 'Wonderwall', pp 78–9 and 80–1.) Built of recycled and recyclable materials, flexible and adaptive in design, with low total lifecycle costs, these structures provide the way forward for a greener city through the creation of sustainable commercial buildings and housing. To truly sustain a city, though, they must also provide food. The loss of allotments in the UK to

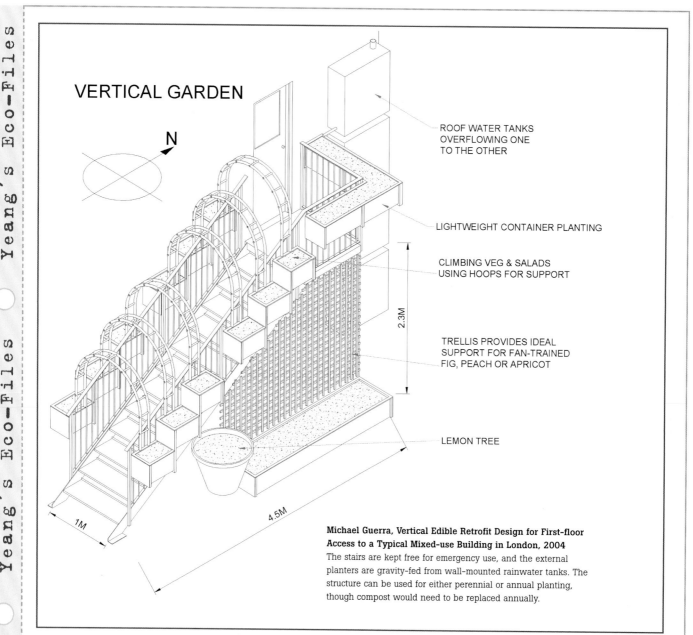

VERTICAL GARDEN

N

ROOF WATER TANKS
OVERFLOWING ONE
TO THE OTHER

LIGHTWEIGHT CONTAINER PLANTING

CLIMBING VEG & SALADS
USING HOOPS FOR SUPPORT

TRELLIS PROVIDES IDEAL
SUPPORT FOR FAN-TRAINED
FIG, PEACH OR APRICOT

2.3M

LEMON TREE

1M

4.5M

**Michael Guerra, Vertical Edible Retrofit Design for First-floor
Access to a Typical Mixed-use Building in London, 2004**
The stairs are kept free for emergency use, and the external
planters are gravity-fed from wall-mounted rainwater tanks. The
structure can be used for either perennial or annual planting,
though compost would need to be replaced annually.

development in the 1980s and 1990s has led to a severe
shortage of land available for local food production. If
modern cities do not address this, there is the very real
threat that they will suffer the same fate as that of ancient
civilisations, such as Lower Mesopotamia and Rome,
which were unable to feed their ever growing populations.

Integrating plants in built structures introduces a
whole new set of design considerations, which are
further intensified by the infrastructure required for
food production. Over thousands of years, agriculture
has worked to optimise the yield, taste and shelf life of
vegetables, fruit and cereals. The effect of this is that
the plants themselves require more light, nutrients,
water and maintenance than a typical houseplant.

New and refurbished buildings must be designed to provide
opportunities for growing food on every surface that has a solar aspect
with access for maintenance and (automatic) watering, while building
in facilities for local composting and incubating seedlings.

Roofs, balconies, external staircases, internal equator-facing atria,
front gardens, back gardens, windows, public spaces, private spaces
and transitional spaces all present opportunities for food production.
They are where people are, and are therefore easy to maintain. Walls
and vertical spaces can also be used as long as provision is made for
access through sliding ladders and walkways. It is also imperative that
the use of land for car parking or long road access is reconsidered. The
thousands of miles given over to hard surfaces for private transport in
cities is a major contributor to urban desertification, pollution and
climate change, adversely impacting global sustainability.

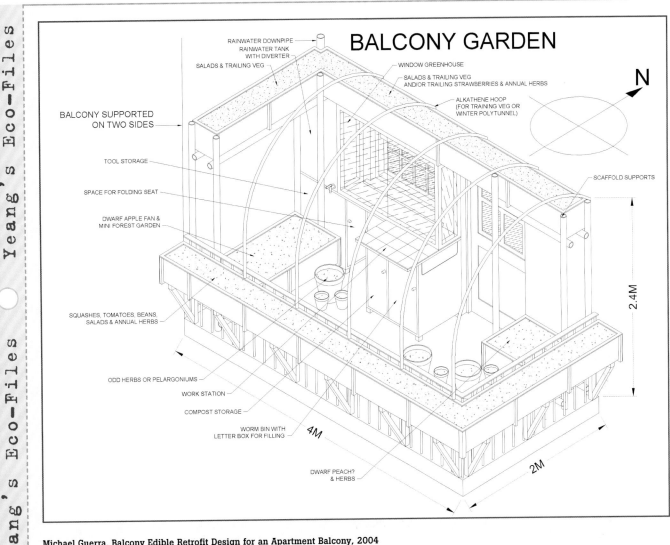

BALCONY GARDEN

RAINWATER DOWNPIPE
RAINWATER TANK
WITH DIVERTER
SALADS & TRAILING VEG

WINDOW GREENHOUSE

SALADS & TRAILING VEG
AND/OR TRAILING STRAWBERRIES & ANNUAL HERBS

ALKATHENE HOOP
(FOR TRAINING VEG OR
WINTER POLYTUNNEL)

N

BALCONY SUPPORTED
ON TWO SIDES

SCAFFOLD SUPPORTS

TOOL STORAGE

SPACE FOR FOLDING SEAT

DWARF APPLE FAN &
MINI FOREST GARDEN

2.4M

SQUASHES, TOMATOES, BEANS,
SALADS & ANNUAL HERBS

ODD HERBS OR PELARGONIUMS

WORK STATION

COMPOST STORAGE

WORM BIN WITH
LETTER BOX FOR FILLING

4M

DWARF PEACH?
& HERBS

2M

Michael Guerra, Balcony Edible Retrofit Design for an Apartment Balcony, 2004
Lightweight planters are used on the edge of the cantilever, while heavier planters for perennials and a
rainwater tank are fixed to the main structure. Arched supports are used for climbers and can be used for
removable glazing in winter for season extending. High-level planters are only used in unshaded positions.

In a post-oil economy, basic nutrition will be the greatest challenge for urban sustainability; it is only the freshest, most local food that has the highest nutritional value. Without oil, multi-storey farms will even find it difficult to support current population densities in cities. While developers seek to maximise their return by maximising density, such an approach in this context could be an ecological liability. Taking the long-term view, developers need to be looking at maximising their return by supporting maximum sustainability. Building Integrated Food Production currently provides developers with a Unique Selling Point as more of the population is increasingly keen to grow their own; it could, though, turn into an Essential Selling Point as growing fresh food becomes not only desirable but necessary. $\varDelta$+

Michael Guerra is an urban permaculture designer and a design engineer who was recently involved in the redevelopment project for St Pancras International Station in London. He is the author of *The Edible Container Garden: Fresh Food from Tiny Spaces* (Gaia Books, 2000).

Ken Yeang is a director of Llewelyn Davies Yeang in London and TR Hamzah & Yeang, its sister company, in Kuala Lumpur, Malaysia. He is the author of many articles and books on sustainable design, including *Ecodesign: A Manual for Ecological Design* (Wiley-Academy 2006).

Notes
1. http://www.fao.org/foodclimate/conference/en/
2. http://www.guerrillagardening.org/
3. www.farmgarden.org.uk/london-pages.html
4. Ken Yeang is an important pioneer of this movement and has been publishing articles on the subject in *AD* since the early 1970s.

McLean's Nuggets

Keeping an Ear Out

Tony Schwartz (1923–2008) was an advertising executive, an audio documentarian and an author, and he became *the* person to go to if you were seeking election or re-election in the US. More interested in the aural potential and information delivery of the radio than the visual entertainment of the television, he became an expert in the political advertisement 'spot'. Talking to *Washington Post* writer Tom Shales in 1983, he said: 'The best thing about radio is that people were born without earlids ... You can't close your ears to it.'[1] In his book *The Responsive Chord* he maintained: 'The best political commercials are Rorschach patterns, they do not tell the viewer anything. They surface his feelings and provide a context for him to express these feelings.'[2] This was a theme developed in the book, where communication is not what I say ... it is what you hear; where he would use what he called 'presearch' (not research) to create the striking of a chord, the chiming of an idea, or the 'tuning in' to a kind of empathetic resonance. The means he used were wide ranging, from the 'political' shaming of irresponsible corporations to the exquisitely recorded bubbles and crackling of Coca-Cola being poured over ice. He was dedicated to the world of sounds, and that unique acoustic and linguistic relationship we have with our environment was documented in a radio show called 'Around NY', which he produced and hosted from 1945 to 1976. He released numerous recordings on Moses Asch's record label Folkways (latterly Smithsonian Folkways) and produced what must have been one of the first 'world music' compilations entitled *The World in My Mailbox*, containing music and sounds from around the world from magnetic-tape recordings that he had exchanged by post. As an expert in the political ad, who played host to such figures as Martin Luther King Jr, Jimmy Carter and Bill Clinton in his Hell's Kitchen recording studio/apartment in NYC's Westside, in the mid-1990s Schwartz was asked by BBC's 'Newsnight' programme to produce a political broadcast for an upcoming US election. His non-partisan but powerful message was merely to vote, because with only half of the potential US voters registered, only half again voting, and about half of them voting for the eventual winners, the notion of democracy becomes stretched extremely thin.

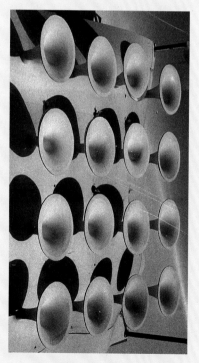

Will McLean, 'Tunable' exponential sonic surface, 1993.

A Note from My Sponsor

A recent invitation to the launch of the annual competition for over-engineered structures at London's Serpentine Gallery included the logotypes of no less than 23 companies who do not seem in immediate need of cut-price publicity. The trend for the endless thanking for the cash or 'in kind' help with media-partnered plugging, printed signboards and plaques, and associated (less than editorially objective) publications continues. While designers struggle with the utterly inconsistent idiosyncrasies of a slew of company logos on a single page, what price the selective removal of such visual spam? FC Barcelona was the last big soccer team in Europe to don shirts without the additional visual paraphernalia of a company logo, other than their own team badge and motto 'more than a club'. In 2006 they finally succumbed in placing UNICEF's (the UN's charity for children) logo on their shirt; arguably more socially useful than flogging an airline or insurer, and certainly less lucrative in the short term with Barcelona actually making a donation to the charity. Do not, though, confuse my reservation about the proliferation of the logo page with distaste for visual stimuli. In designer Mark Boyce's excellent new book *Sizes May Vary: A Workbook for Graphic Designers*,[3] he includes an exhaustively dimensioned set of spaces in which to feature information design and the advertisement, from the standardised dimensions of saleable space in a magazine to that of the large-scale roadside billboard.

Let's Get Small

Speaking his highly specific brand of Californian Scottish, Professor James Gimzewski delivered the first joint IET/IoN (Institution of Engineering and Technology/Institute of Nanotechnology) lecture.[4] Gimzewski made his name as part of a team at IBM Zurich that utilised the Scanning Tunnel Microscope to study and manipulate surface morphology at an atomic scale. His talk, entitled 'The Age of Nanotechnology', articulated this new meta-disciplinary science, whose commonality is that of scale – the nano scale. If this scale is hard to envision, to which Gimzewski will attest, then the use of engineering 1:1000 measurement systems are useful. He illustrated three steps of a factor of 1,000: the first, the image of an ant measured in millimetres, the second the image of a cell measured in micrometres, and thirdly the image of a virus, measured in nanometres (nm). To clarify, a nanometre is a billionth of a metre, and a C60 carbon molecule (more commonly known as a Buckminster Fullerene, or Buckyball) is 1 nm in diameter. Utilising the technology of the nano scale, Gimzewski sees multivalent possibilities for a new type of designable matter for any number of applications. His work as Professor of Chemistry at UCLA concentrates on medical applications, but the physical disposition of his new facility, the California NanoSystems Institute, attests to the cross-disciplinary nature of their work, which may as easily look at a coating on a golf ball assisting a straight-line trajectory or the treatment of specific cancers. Gimzewski declared during his talk that in comparison with microelectronics, 'medical technology is in the stone-age'. He detailed how the NanoSystems Institute's experiments

with nano treatments could alter the Young's Modulus (or stickiness) of cancerous cells to prevent their potential spread to other parts of the body. Nanotechnology is a new science and it and the cytoarchitecture of Gimzewski's experiments were, he said, 'in their infancy'. The proliferation of nanotechnology, though, is in no doubt, and the excellent textile trade magazine *Future Materials* recently featured articles on improving the efficiency of the thermoelectric effect (the conversion of heat into electricity and its reciprocal operation) to obtain energy from the waste heat from car exhausts, and numerous nano-coatings for self-cleaning, anti-microbial and antistatic effects.[5] Gimzewski said he saw a new kind of revolution in fabrication that replaces the 'heat, beat and treat' technologies of the past, and that transcends the unhelpful distinction between branches of science and the sciences, arts and humanities. In a recent paper entitled 'Nanotechnology: The Endgame of Materialism', he talks about how 'nanotechnological evolution will lead to a total hybridism of mind–machine and art–science and new forms of personal interrelationship'.[6] ⏀+

Depiction of Hare's ratio, which illustrates the relative size of a Buckyball, a football and spaceship Earth. Produced by Dr Jonathan P Hare as part of his work with the Creative Science Centre (www.creative-science.org.uk) to promote and enthuse the creative potential of science.

'McLean's Nuggets' is an ongoing technical series inspired by Will McLean and Samantha Hardingham's enthusiasm for back issues of *AD*, as explicitly explored in Hardingham's *AD* issue *The 1970s is Here and Now* (March/April 2005).

Will McLean is joint coordinator of technical studies (with Pete Silver) in the Department of Architecture at the University of Westminster. He recently co-authored, also with Pete Silver, the book *Introduction to Architectural Technology* (Laurence King, 2008).

Notes
1. Republished in his obituary, *Washington Post*, 17 June 2008.
2. Tony Schwartz, *The Responsive Chord*, Anchor Press (New York), 1973, p 72.
3. Mark Boyce, *Sizes May Vary: A Workbook for Graphic Designers*, Laurence King (London), 2008.
4. 'The Age of Nanotechnology', lecture given by Professor Gimzewski at the Institute of Engineering and Technology, Savoy Place, London, 8 July 2008.
5. *Future Materials*, June 2008, World Textile Publications (Bradford, UK). http://www.world-textile.net.
6. Professor James Gimzewski, 'Nanotechnology: The Endgame of Materialism', *Leonardo*, Vol 41, No 3, pp 259–64, 2008.

Kalmar Museum of Art

Timothy Tore Hebb describes a new intervention by Tham & Videgård Hansson (TVH) in the medieval city of Kalmar in southeast Sweden. He describes how the 'black box' form of the museum is a metaphor for the contemporary situation while also responding innovatively to its historic setting.

Tham & Videgård Hansson, Kalmar Museum of Art, Kalmar, Sweden, 2008
Hidden among the greenery of the park the black, four-storey cube carefully reveals itself to visitors as they approach the museum.

The design by Tham & Videgård Hansson (TVH) for a new museum of art at Kalmar encountered strong opposition from many locals. The City Park, where the new building is located, is considered an important public space by many of the city's inhabitants, and there were fears that a new contemporary building would interfere with the historic setting, which has had no new architecture since the 1950s, and change the medieval identity of this small city with a population of just 65,000.

In May 2008, after almost two years on site, the new museum was finally inaugurated.

Situated on the Baltic coast and near to the border with Denmark, Kalmar was one of Sweden's most important cities from the 13th to the 17th century. It has one of the best-preserved Renaissance castles in northern Europe, as well as Storkyrkan Cathedral, which was built by Nicodemus Tessin the Elder, the architect of the royal castle in Stockholm. The new landmark building, however, provides a bridge between the city's prestigious past and the more uncertain and complex challenges of its future.

Moreover, the modest, black-box shape of the museum contains many narratives that today pose urgent and timeless questions regarding the future survival of man. Its entirely concrete form with tight and fortress-like windows could be interpreted as dealing with the fear most of us feel about the consequences of a changing climate, and perhaps also with the risk of nuclear terrorism.

A black box, rectangular in shape, also calls to mind the pilots' last discussion before the crash, or a world where oil is rapidly diminishing, or a black hole in space that could swallow up everything, as well as referring back to a medieval watchtower. All in all, a beacon calling out to the world for reason. Threats and potential disasters seem to be coming at us from all directions these days, and these need to be met and resolved. Yet the museum, both inside and out, does not feel dark and hopeless: it is full of energy and opportunities.

When asked about the foreboding shape and skin of the building, the architects' response was that it was all in the eye of the beholder. They did not have medieval or Renaissance architecture in mind when they designed the project, instead focusing on the use of light and the building's connection with its surroundings.

Bolle Tham and Martin Videgård, the principals of TVH, are both graduates of the KTH School of Architecture in Stockholm. Since they established their office in the city in 1999, they have alternated between practice and teaching at architecture schools in Sweden and abroad. Their reputation has been built mainly on their domestic work; for example, the rethinking of the villa, using building techniques and shapes in new ways. With an interest in matching the quality and detailing of traditional craftsmanship with industrial building processes, their villas are constructed from wood and in situ cast concrete using computed-aided design tools.

The international competition to design the Kalmar Museum of Art attracted 294 proposals. However, the jury particularly liked TVH's design solution, which combined the interaction of a contemporary structure with the historic City Park, well-conceived exhibition spaces and the unusual manipulation of interior light: the second-floor wall, which faces the park, can be totally removed to reveal a large window that can fill the interior space, for contemporary exhibits, with light and at the same time offer glorious views of the park, and the roof is made partially out of transparent glass, bathing the fourth floor in natural light.

'In this context, we wanted to create a building with a strong identity that can hide among the leaves. The exterior surface is covered with dark, large-scale wooden panels, enhanced to bring out the wood vein. Inside, walking vertically up four levels gives people new ways of looking at the park, city and lake,' explains Tham.

The height of the museum was determined, to some extent, by the limited site. The whole building is made out of in situ cast concrete and the interior walls are mainly especially fine and light Portland cement – a choice made together with the director of the museum. It was also necessary to connect the museum's volume to the adjacent restaurant pavilion, which was designed in the 1930s by the well-known Modernist architect Sven-Ivar Lind. In doing so, the architects have created a striking contrast between the enigmatic black box and Lind's functionalist building that produces a new kind of energy that feels right for today's Kalmar and gives it 'the makings of a big city', as the city's website boasts. 𝟃+

Timothy Tore Hebb is an author who writes mainly on Swedish architecture and industrial design, often focusing on how the needs of man and society in general can be met through design. His articles have been published in the Swedish morning daily *Dagens Nyheter* and leading Swedish architecture magazine *Arkitektur*.

On the fourth floor, northern light enters zig-zag light shafts, doubling the ceiling height up to about 8 metres (26.2 feet). The space is reserved for the museum's collection of modern art.

Architectural Design **New Urban China** September/October 2008

What is Architectural Design?

Launched in 1930, *Architectural Design* is an influential and prestigious architectural publication. With an almost unrivalled reputation worldwide, it is consistently at the forefront of cultural thought and design.

Architectural Design is published bimonthly. Features include:

Main section

The main section of every issue functions as a book and is guest-edited by a leading international expert in the field.

△+

The △+ magazine section at the back of every issue includes ongoing series and regular columns.

Truly international in terms of the subjects covered and its contributors, *Architectural Design*:

- focuses on cutting-edge design
- combines the currency and topicality of a newsstand journal with the rigour and production qualities of a book
- is provocative and inspirational, inspiring theoretical, creative and technological advances
- questions the outcomes of technical innovations as well as the far-reaching social, cultural and environmental challenges that present themselves today

How to Subscribe

With 6 issues a year, you can subscribe to △ (either print or online), or buy titles individually.

Subscribe today to receive 6 issues delivered direct to your door!

£198 / US$369	institutional subscription (combined print and online)
£180 / US$335	institutional subscription (print or online)
£110 / US$170	personal rate subscription (print only)
£70 / US$110	student rate subscription (print only)

To subscribe: Tel: +44 (0) 843 828
                 Email: cs-journals@wiley.com

To purchase individual titles go to:
           www.wiley.com

Made in India, guest-edited by Kazi K Ashraf, is the recipient of the Pierre Vago Journalism Award 2008, awarded by the CICA International Book Awards